How to Think Things

and Other Useful Tips

A.J. Moroney

To my Father, for teaching me to think deeply

To my Mother, for teaching me the value of truth

To Nicci, for walking beside me

To Zeke and Saoirse, for no reason at all, except that I
adore them

Preface

"Opening your book with a quote demonstrates that you are not alone in your intellectual position, and that you have a respect for tradition and the ideas of your predecessors. All of this is completely undercut, though, if you happen to be quoting yourself." - A.J. Moroney

In (almost) all seriousness, while I will unabashedly demonstrate my willingness to bring levity in wherever I can, I do feel as though I have an important reason for writing this book. The problem, as I see it, is that we have lost the ability to communicate productively with one another. I believe this is a symptom of the deeper and more insidious problem that we have largely lost track of how to think. The speakers aren't saying things clearly because their ideas are unclear, and the listeners aren't inclined to really listen anyway, so how can we expect to understand one another?

As writing is itself a form of this ill-fated communication, I expect many of you will already see my dilemma. I find myself in the undesirable position of writing a book that attempts to explain the best way to read a book. The problem that follows is that I think many people who read this book will have a tendency to misunderstand me for the very reasons I think this book is necessary. (I should warn you, this is hardly the last time we'll find ourselves in such a paradoxical position.)

As we proceed, I will try very hard never to say a thing is true unless it is either obvious in itself, or I have done my best to adequately support my claim, but here I must ask you to indulge me in a few ways as we begin. In a sense, I'm asking you to participate in an experiment. My hope is that you will have very good reasons to accept the following guidelines by the time you've finished reading this book, but as you are unlikely to have saved the preface for last, for now I'm afraid I must ask you to do the following things as an unmerited favor.

First, please try your best not to think about who I am. Focus on the ideas instead. I'm fighting very hard against the temptation to tell you all the ways in which I feel I am or am not qualified to say the things I am about to say, but none of that matters. I know that many of you have been trained, as I have, to try and understand who an author is in order to frame what they write. But whatever you might glean about me from what I've written in this book will leave you with a vague, and probably inaccurate impression of who I am. More importantly, who I am is irrelevant if you can determine whether or not what I'm saying is true. If a true statement is said with nefarious intentions, that doesn't make it any less true, and a false statement declared with the noblest of intentions isn't any less false. Whether you find my mannerisms charming or repulsive, or whether you suspect my motives to be heroic or villainous, if the way you feel about me as a person steers you at all, it will have steered you wrong.

Second, please begin with skepticism, if you feel so inclined, but don't be content to remain there. While I think skepticism may be a favorable extreme to naïveté, merely listening doesn't always amount to actually understanding—particularly when you're listening with an inclination toward distrust—and you'll never arrive at anything resembling real knowledge if you're ever the skeptic. Skepticism for its own sake is a natural enemy of knowledge. If you never believe anything, you'll never know anything, and if you can't know anything, then this book (like all other books, I suppose) will be a waste of your time. You will not be able to learn that I am right, or that I am wrong, if you maintain a position of absolute skepticism. I would be much happier if you learned that I was wrong than if you learned nothing at all. It's taken an awfully long time to write all of this down, and it will likely take you quite a long time to read it as well; it would be a dreadful waste if no one learned anything in the end.

Third, please think carefully about what you read. And I don't just mean think critically (although I do mean that as well), I mean do your best to think with precision and clarity. Try to assume as little as you can, and try to make sure my meaning is clear to you before moving on. Obviously if I am unclear in what I say it doesn't matter how clearly you consider it, but you will also miss my meaning if you read this book without keeping your expectations in check. If you assume I am going to say something, you will likely hear it, whether I say it or not. If you assume I am not going to say something, you may miss it when I do. I'm sure you must know this, as I do, from experience. It is hard to listen well. But unfortunately this book is riddled with subtle, but important distinctions which will have implications beyond what you might expect later in the book. If you don't take the time to really understand some of the things we discuss, especially near the beginning, much of what I say later on may seem foolish. You may think me foolish in the end anyway, but why not at least start out on the right foot?

Finally, I feel I must inform you that I am a Christian. I'm not telling you this because I think it will help you understand what I say. In fact, I'm quite sure that for many people it will have the opposite effect. Some people will tend to accept what I say without really thinking about it because they believe what I believe, and others will tend to dismiss what I say because they do not. I am only telling you this so that no one gets to the end of this book and feels as though the rug has been pulled out from under them. Much of the fourth part of this book involves demonstrating the principles of "good thinking" applied to the most basic observations we can make as human beings. I believe that most probably leads to the idea that something very much like the Judeo-Christian God exists. It is only a demonstration, though, and for the most part the principles discussed still stand without it. If it offends you, skip it. But I think any discussion of truth is hollow without relevance, and I can't think of anything that could be more relevant to a person in this universe than the infinite and the eternal. If you agree that it is a worthwhile discussion, please read it, I hope you will enjoy it. If you don't, please ignore it. You won't have offended me, and I trust you can find your own applications for the ideas in this book.

Part 1: Truth

How do you know?

Why do you believe the things you believe?

Have you ever sat down and thought about it? There are all sorts of answers one might very reasonably give to that question, but broadly speaking the only reason anyone believes anything is because (as far as they can tell) that thing is true. There is sometimes an element of choice that steers a person along the path toward a belief, particularly if there is no truly compelling evidence one way or another. Other times the evidence is so inescapably conclusive that you've adopted the belief before you're aware there was any opportunity to disbelieve in the first place. In any case, though, no matter how hard you try, you can never really believe something you know to be false.

This is important because a person's beliefs are a driving force behind every deliberate action they take, no matter how inconsequential it may seem. If I believe I will be more comfortable if it's warmer, then I might turn up the thermostat. If I believe a ham sandwich will be delicious, I might choose to eat one for lunch. And as I'm sure you're aware, sometimes our beliefs have enormous consequences. If I believe that human beings have essential worth, I might make sacrifices to feed the poor. If I believe that life is ultimately meaningless, I might become a tyrant who oppresses them instead.

If you are at all concerned with doing the right things, then, it follows that it is incredibly important to have the right beliefs. But of course the phrase "the right beliefs" begs so many questions that it's hard to know where to begin. If we trace things backward it becomes a little clearer. If your actions are guided by your beliefs, and your beliefs are determined by what you think is true, then the important thing is the ability to accurately determine what's true. So if you want to do the right things, your beliefs must align with reality. Much more simply put (and I doubt this will come as a surprise to anyone), we need to avoid being wrong.

In my own abundant experience with being wrong, the reason is most often somewhere on the spectrum between an honest mistake and willful ignorance. Willful ignorance can happen for all sorts of reasons, but in this book we're going to concern ourselves with how to avoid honestly believing something that isn't true, and there are really only two avenues toward that irksome and unpleasant destination. The first is a faulty assumption.

Everything you believe either is or begins with a basic, foundational assumption: a belief you have that you can prove, or that must be true in itself. Logicians call this foundational assumption a premise. We're capable of discovering and understanding complex facts and ideas because we combine those simple premises to form more complex conclusions. Those conclusions can then be used as premises to support even more complex conclusions. Even the most complicated beliefs you hold can be traced back to simple assumptions that you combined to construct a framework capable of supporting rich and meaningful knowledge. As a consequence, if one of those simple assumptions is faulty, it can have drastic effects on beliefs which may seem to be entirely unrelated.

At a glance the statement that all of your beliefs depend on a smallish set of simple assumptions might seem sorely misguided. If it doesn't, feel free to skip ahead a bit, but we'll need to agree here if you're going to get anything out of the rest of this book, so I'll spend some time explaining what I mean.

It's true that sometimes the chains of premises supporting an idea are immensely long and interwoven, making it difficult to discern any one thread. To further complicate things, assumptions that you're unaware of can leave you with the feeling that you "just know" something. Careful examination of any belief you have, though, will eventually take you back to a list of simple premises that form its foundation. That's the only way to move from simple facts and observations, like "I exist," or "things fall," to more complex beliefs like "I have a purpose," or "gravity is a force between objects."

These foundational premises are, by necessity, either true in themselves, or true in a directly demonstrable way, without needing to depend on other facts to prop them up. Descartes' famous "I think therefore I am," for example, begins with the demonstrable fact that Descartes was capable of thinking (if he wasn't he wouldn't have been able to tell us so), and since someone must exist in order do anything, including thinking, he's able to infer that he must, in fact, exist. Or you might make a statement like "I'm hungry." You don't really need to qualify that statement, because you're able to directly observe your own sensations. But these foundational premises aren't usually very useful by themselves. Knowing that you exist and that you're hungry is all well and good, but knowing how to get a free lunch is a lot more helpful, and you'll need to connect a few more dots in order to figure that out.

At the risk of belaboring the point, let's examine a statement that seems simple and obvious, like "my Mom loves me." It's one of those things—at least for those fortunate enough to have loving mothers—that doesn't seem like it requires any philosophical underpinnings. It's just a simple, undeniable fact. But let's work backward and ask that age-old question (and the bane of every 7-year-old's parents): "How do you know?"

One of the more obvious ways I might know my Mom loves me is through observation. We see and hear her doing things that a loving person would do, and if it walks like a duck and quacks like a duck that loves its ducklings, it probably is. But what if we can't trust our senses? On closer inspection we realize we're still depending on ideas that we haven't consciously brought into the equation yet. For example, if you recall what I wrote about Descartes, you may have noticed that in order for my Mother to love (or do anything at all) she must exist. So one premise of the belief that "my Mom loves me" might be "my Mom exists." If we assume we can trust our senses then that part's easy enough; we'd have a lot of trouble seeing or hearing her if she didn't exist. But you may have gotten ahead of me and noticed that we still don't have enough information to bridge the gap between what we know and what we want to prove. We might very reasonably say "she loves, therefore she is," but the inverse argument, "she is, therefore she loves," is much more dubious. For instance, we also have to assert that beings which exist are capable of love. And that's not necessarily true of all beings, is it? Do single-celled organisms count as beings? Are they capable of love? How exactly do we define "beings"? And how exactly do we define "love"? A particular shade of faulty assumption threatens to creep in and make things difficult for us—imprecise definitions can derail even the sturdiest trains of thought. But even with clearly defined terms, when you start to really examine ideas in this way it can quickly reach a point where you start wondering just how deep the rabbit hole goes.

But while the path from premise to conclusion can be long and hazardous, if you're able to avoid the various pitfalls when constructing and combining your ideas, then by inferring from the relationships between facts you're able to move all the way from ideas as simple and seemingly inconsequential as "my Mother and I exist," and "existent beings are sometimes capable of love," to a much more complex, meaningful and useful statement, like "my Mother loves me."

The ice gets a bit thinner, though, because the more complicated an idea is, in a way, the more fragile it is. The trouble is that those chains of premises we're using to support our conclusions may fail if even one of the links is faulty. All it takes is a single false premise to bring even the mightiest conclusion crashing down into a useless heap of rubble. And most of the really important ideas are much more complicated than they may seem at first.

If you're one of those exceptional (or exceptionally bored) people who reads the preface, this is why it's so important to do the "careful thinking" I briefly mentioned there. Thinking "critically" as I and many others were taught scratches the surface of these concepts. We're told about the importance of identifying biases (emotionally driven assumptions), and fact-checking the author of an essay, for example, but we seem to gloss over or take for granted the *means* by which we can assess assumptions, or why it's so important that the author's facts (premises) are true to begin with.

Once you understand, though, that at its core every affirmative idea we have is a tower of cards, not only is it obvious why we need to check facts and challenge assumptions, it is immediately clear that we need to go all the way down to the base to really see how solid the idea is.

And that's the really important thing I want to establish; if the base isn't solid, nothing built on top of it will hold any weight. We've been working backward, or upside down, because the importance of the fundamental assumptions is so often understated or ignored, but if we've established how important the foundation is we can start looking at it the right way up. We can start at the bottom, and work our way toward the top.

It's down at the lowest levels of our mental frameworks where the really crucial work is done. The base of the tower supporting each idea in a person's mind is what philosophers often refer to as a "worldview." It's a lens through which a person processes ideas. Your worldview is a set of assumptions —often so deeply held that you're barely aware of them—

which form the foundation for all of your beliefs. Since these ideas form the foundation of the tower, they're ultimately the most important. If you've got a crumbling brick halfway up a tower you might lose everything above it in a storm, but you'll still have something solid to rebuild upon. If the foundation can't be depended upon, though, it's unlikely there will be anything left standing after the wind and rain are done howling. In building, as in thinking, if your foundation isn't firm then little else matters. How well your roof keeps out the rain is irrelevant if it ends up covering a pile of rubble instead of your living room.

As you might expect, though, repairing a foundation usually means digging up things that have been buried for a long time—some of which you may have forgotten were there at all. In the same way that an archeologist comes to a new understanding of something forgotten, this business of repairing deeply buried things usually involves some element of investigation and discovery. And even once you've discovered the areas of your foundation that need rethinking, the trouble is compounded by the fact that there are usually important things built on top of a foundation, and those things will very often need to be removed or rebuilt along with the foundational elements they depend upon. All of this to say it is not a task you can take lightly if you mean to really do it well. But with a solid foundation, in the end you will be able to build much higher, and much stronger, than you ever could without one. So while it's difficult, and sometimes tedious work digging up and repairing the foundation, it's work that's well worth doing in the long run.

If all of this talk of hard, tedious work has discouraged you, it may help if I pause here and clarify something. I may have given the impression until now that I think you should fully examine every premise that supports an idea every time you consider anything, but that's not really what I mean to say. When you're hanging something on a wall, (if you'll forgive my overuse of the construction metaphor) you might need to make sure you're nailing into a solid part of the wall, but you wouldn't tear the whole wall apart to see how it's sitting on the floor. If your house was built well, the work of ensuring the walls are solid in the way they join and depend upon the floor (and the floor on the foundation beneath that) has already been done. If the work is done well, it usually only needs to be done once. The problem with the current state of affairs is that so many of us are trying to hang pictures in houses that were constructed by misguided contractors, and we're left scratching our heads when the entire wall falls over at the first swing of the hammer.

Very little of my experience in education ever asked me to think about how to build the foundation. We spent a lot of time on the walls, and quite a lot more time than I think was necessary on some of the more decorative bits, but all the while we were building on a foundation that was riddled with gaps and weak points that no one ever called any attention to. We laid some rather lovely flooring, and by the time I realized I had a problem the really dangerous parts were well and truly hidden. It took quite a bit of tearing up and redoing work (even work that was initially well done, given the circumstances) before the house was ready to support its own weight. Sadly, many of us find ourselves in this position. Though the work is hard, and you're never paid for it up front, there's simply no way around it. We must dig up the forgotten assumptions we buried long ago, discard and replace the broken parts, and then begin rebuilding with a sure foundation.

So then, now that we've completed the architectural master class and thoroughly abused a perfectly good metaphor, let's begin examining those foundations.

How to think things

If we're going to be rethinking our core assumptions, it seems to me the best way to begin is by figuring out the best way to think. In a general sense, saying there is a "best" way is a bit misleading, since there are obviously plenty of perfectly good ways to think. The best way to think about composing a symphony, though, differs sharply from the way you might want to think about studying geology. While there's tremendous value in the type of thinking that involves creativity and imagination, I'm sorry to say we're primarily concerned with the geology-type thinking in this part of the book. What I mean is thinking which is purely concerned with facts—which is to say thinking which solely and directly pertains to truth. I hope I haven't said anything to disparage geologists, but most of us don't find that sort of thinking particularly entertaining. And even if you find yourself among the lucky few that do, I don't believe the majority of our thinking should bother much with examining the truth directly in the dry, academic sense anyway. Things like love, kindness and gratitude should enter our minds without careful consideration, and the entire point of creativity is to consider things which aren't yet real, and therefore aren't yet true. It can be incredibly useful, and often incredibly fulfilling, to think in terms of what could be instead of thinking in terms of what is. But all of these abstract forms of thinking draw energy and stability from the "foundation" we discussed in the first chapter.

What I mean is that if you take time to discover the deeper realities about the people around you, love and kindness will thereafter come much more naturally, and much more frequently to your mind. If you take time to understand how fortunate you really are to have the things you have, gratitude will remain at the forefront of your mind with much less effort on your part. And if creativity is to do anything more than provide you with a respite from the types of thought you find less interesting, then it too will need some grounding in what's real and true.

There are places in your mind where no one can go except you, but reality, and therefore truth, is the plane we share. So the best (or at least most helpful) creative endeavors are the ones that take something real and true, bring it into the abstract world within the mind, then shift it, spin it, decorate it, and bring it back into the shared realm of reality so others can see it with fresh eyes, or from a different angle than they had before. A meaningful understanding of what could be requires a solid understanding of what is. Otherwise your intellectual ventures aren't likely to accomplish more than keeping you entertained for a moment. When diving into abstract worlds, knowing what's true gives you an idea of where to start, and if you're going to be helpful to anyone else by venturing where no one can follow you, you'd better keep in mind the way back. So while I don't think anyone should spend all of their time thinking directly about plain, foundational truth, you'll do much better in your other mental endeavors if you think carefully about it at least once before moving on to anything else.

Whatever the reasons for avoiding the deep and dry territories of unembellished truth, I think most of us miss how deeply important "good thinking" really is. In fact I'm not sure many of us are even aware that we think in a particular way, let alone whether our way of thinking might be called good or bad —although interestingly, we tend to be very quick to point out bad thinking in others even if we haven't figured out what good thinking looks like for ourselves.

During most of our education, we're almost constantly told what to think about, but we're usually given far less guidance on how to think about it. Mathematics (and science to some degree) is something of an exception, in that one is often required to "show their work." But even then, to me it generally seemed to be more about memorizing a method than really gaining a genuine understanding. Or at least I never got the impression that the system as a whole (not to say anything necessarily about individual teachers) cared at all whether I really understood why a certain formula was helpful for solving a certain kind of problem, so long as I could remember which formulas went with which problems. I was asked to remember quite a few things (most of which I've probably forgotten by now), but I was rarely asked to genuinely understand.

I imagine many of our education systems were designed by incredibly practical people. And the approach does make a good deal of sense in light of the fact that a person's ability to make a living for themselves will almost always be more closely related to what they are able to do, not merely what they understand. Perhaps consequently, there seems to be an unyielding focus on building skills above all else. You must be able to read, write, add, subtract, recite the periodic table, and develop the ability to do any number of other things, but questions of purpose are often entirely neglected.

There's a terrible sort of pragmatism in a system which asks you to learn the how, without ever taking the time to examine the why. As I write this, it almost sounds as though I'm describing an oppressive system of control, designed to create an unquestioning populace that still manages to be productive at generating wealth for the ruling class. In fact it seems a cold and jagged version of that philosophy was applied under the Nazi regime in the 1930's. Gregor Ziemer said in *Education for Death* (an examination of schools in Nazi Germany) that "Physical education, education for action, is alone worthy of the Nazi teacher's attention. All else can be dismissed as non-essential . . ." I'm not much of a historian, but I imagine something very much like that ideology has likely been applied to education under other despots as well.

But obviously that's a rather extreme example. Most modern systems of education I'm aware of don't take nearly so hard a stance against questions of purpose. I believe in most cases our education systems are invented by well meaning individuals—possibly some who have lived through their own hardship lacking marketable skills in a world that too often seems concerned with little else besides what each person has to offer. It seems entirely possible to me that those who helped create such education systems as I endured might have done so with a genuine desire to equip students to make the most of their adult lives. Perhaps it isn't that they had any intention to quash questions of purpose, but merely that those questions seemed comparatively less important than the development of skills.

But whatever their intentions may have been (I can only guess), teaching the how without teaching the why is shortsighted. If all you require of students is memorizing methods, you'll be left with an entire generation that is incapable of grasping the value of true understanding, to the detriment of the students, and to the benefit of anyone who may wish to take advantage of them.

It goes a bit deeper, though, because the critical flaw as it pertained to me personally was that whether understanding was required of me or not, I was never really provided with the tools that the task of understanding required. People seemed to talk endlessly about knowledge, but no one ever mentioned truth. That's the part I didn't really add up until later. I was under the impression that someone who remembered a lot of things was knowledgeable by definition—but that implicitly assumes that everything you remember is true. Knowledge wasn't properly defined. We say we "know" something because we heard it from a professor, or we read it in a book, but knowledge isn't really knowledge at all unless what's in your head corresponds with reality. The really important thing, then, isn't gaining "knowledge" (in that sense), it's discerning truth.

I must have heard the maxim "knowledge is power" dozens, or even hundreds of times before I made it through my education, and I think it's true, but only if you apply a very particular definition of knowledge. In fact I think it would be much clearer to say "truth is power." Memorization isn't power at all in itself, and it can only lead you to power if the things you memorize are true, and you understand how and when to apply them. Building a skill certainly creates a kind of power, but it is a power without purpose by itself. A person who has the capability to do something, but doesn't understand why or when that skill should be used, is effectively an automaton—a mere tool. And the real power of a tool is in the hands of the person using it, not in the tool itself. Discovering and understanding truth, as opposed to merely memorizing disconnected facts, is the only real means of harnessing power. It is the only way you will be able to reliably make use of power for anything other than destruction. Power without purpose can be a truly dreadful thing.

So, if there is no substitute for the complete truth (or as much of it as we can ascertain), then as I've suggested several times already, answering the question "how should one think?" really boils down to "how can one determine what's true?". In fact, if you had asked me to succinctly describe "how to think things," I would say you should find a way to keep your mind pointed squarely at the truth. Everything else will fall into place. The thoughts you think will be useful and relevant, because what's true is what's real, and reality is where you live. The thoughts you think will be coherent with each other, because they will all correlate with a coherent reality. The thoughts you think will consistently drive you toward a deeper and more meaningful understanding, which is to say genuine knowledge, which is to say true power, which is to say the capacity to improve the lives of everyone around you. Naturally your mind will wander in all sorts of directions chasing after whims and fantasies, but if you can manage to remember that your ultimate destination is the truth, you will never be lost for long.

But of course if recognizing truth were as straightforward as it sounds, I shouldn't have bothered writing this book. There are plenty of hidden gems and secret paths to uncover on the road ahead, but there are pitfalls we should avoid as well. I said I was rarely exposed to any direct training on how to think the right way, but as anyone who's ever tried to assemble a piece of furniture without reading the instructions will likely be able to tell you, not learning the right way usually means learning several wrong ways. There are several of these "wrong ways" that I believe many of us have learned during our education, and which I fear too few of us have unlearned.

A lot of what follows will be, in some ways, stated in the negative. In fact I considered titling this book "How Not to Think Things" at one point. In part that's because my personal journey involved finding a lot of bad ways to think before I found any good ones. It's also because I find it far easier to be a critic than it is to put forward original ideas. But if this book can truly be called educational in any sense, it must be a reeducation. You couldn't have become literate enough to read this book without making decisions about how to think. If you were given some of the same guidance I was, then improving your ability to think clearly will likely involve unlearning nearly as much as it will involve learning. There must usually be a "de-education" before there can be a reeducation.

So there will be a pattern of "not that, but this instead" as we remove some of these troublesome barriers to clear thinking. I will do my best to explain the flaws that are apparent in the ways we very often consider things—especially the most important things. Then I will try and demonstrate what I hope you will agree is a better way. I wouldn't dare to call this a complete guide. For that matter I wouldn't dare to claim that I have this thinking business completely figured out myself. In fact I daresay no mortal person ever has. In my experience, at least, the ones who claim to have "arrived" are usually people who have simply become so proud of themselves for how far they have come that they can no longer see how far they have yet to go. You can "arrive" in that sense easily enough. All a traveler needs to do is stop moving and they will certainly arrive somewhere. But while I can't tell you exactly where the destination is, I will at least endeavor to help you avoid some of the pits I fell into, and share with you the roads which helped me to get somewhere worth being.

Open-mindedness

The first of the roadblocks we'll attempt to dismantle is the idea that a person should *always* be open-minded. I don't remember the last time I heard a talk, or read an article about "good thinking" which didn't suggest (or even insist) that thinking well is practically synonymous with being open-minded. I know to some I may already seem like a rigid, fundamentalist fool for even hinting at the idea that being open-minded may not be all it's cracked up to be, but I believe that is probably because the ways in which open-mindedness can actually be helpful are more subtle and nuanced than they seem.

It would be very easy to overstate what I mean. Dichotomies are simple, and this simplicity makes even the false ones seem attractive. So when speaking out against one extreme, it is often difficult not to seem as though you're endorsing the opposite extreme. So what I intend to say is "open-mindedness is not good," but I feel I should say in the same breath that I don't intend to say "open-mindedness is bad," or even that "closed-mindedness is good." The trouble, as I see it, is not that open-mindedness is encouraged, it's that it is treated as *intrinsically* good, or good in itself.

Open-mindedness is very often treated as the supreme mental virtue. Rigidity, we're told, is the frailty of any system of thought. Modern thinkers are supposed to be adaptive and dynamic, refusing to be pinned down, or to exclude any ideas. Thinking in "black and white" is often scoffed at as an outdated, flawed, and failed way to look at the world. We're taught not only to acknowledge, but to embrace the "gray areas" where it seems there is no real truth. But treating open-mindedness as a universal good without any concern for context or qualification is an oversimplification with dire consequences concerning a person's ability to think clearly. Open-mindedness is incredibly useful when it is treated as a means to an end, but it is utterly useless when it is treated as the pinnacle of human thought.

I want to make sure it's clear, open-mindedness is sometimes indispensable in the honest search for truth. There's an obvious appeal to adaptive thinking, and obvious merit to genuinely considering all ideas. But like nearly all virtues, both become vice in excess. Eating is good, but too much eating will ruin your health. Sleeping is good, but too much sleeping will leave you destitute. Telling the truth is good, but the fact that everything worth saying is true doesn't mean everything true is worth saying. In the same way, flexibility in your thinking is good, but if you never decide firmly whether an idea is right or wrong, you'll never really know anything. And refusing to exclude new ideas is good, but persistently refusing to exclude ideas once you've considered them is ultimately choosing to remain ignorant. Open-mindedness cannot bring you to the truth by itself.

You might think of treating open-mindedness as the goal like trying to build a wall out of clay. Clay has several properties which make it uniquely suited to certain functions. It can take one shape at one time, and be molded and reformed into something else at another time. But it never finds true strength until it is baked and hardened. It doesn't matter what shape you form clay into, it will collapse under any significant load you place on top of it. If you try to build something very tall by placing clay on top of clay, you will generally end up building something wide instead. The malleability of clay allows you to create bricks of just the right size and shape to build higher than you could with many other materials, but unless the clay is hardened it will collapse under its own weight. Similarly, open-mindedness allows you to be malleable and adaptive in your thinking, but if you refuse to affirm that anything is true, you will find yourself stuck in the shallowest pools of thought, unable to climb any higher until you solidify your foundation. If you are flexible in the beginning, you will be stronger in the end, but if you refuse to be inflexible in the end, you will never be strong at all.

That said, I suspect that for many that metaphor will have missed the point. In my experience, at least, this embracing of perpetual "open-mindedness" doesn't usually seem to be directly motivated by a genuine desire to discover the truth. I imagine many will be unconcerned by its shortcomings in this area since they're primarily interested in open-mindedness for the peripheral benefits afforded by avoiding commitment to a belief.

At its worst, using open-mindedness as an excuse to avoid committing to beliefs is simply a form of intellectual laziness; it allows a person to dodge the difficult work of thinking long and hard about complicated or controversial ideas. If an idea causes you any trouble you can just dump it into a "gray area," applaud yourself for being so open-minded, and go about your day. At its best, though, I've seen it motivated by compassion, and an honest (I might even say noble) desire for peace.

Whatever the motivation, many people seem to genuinely believe that we'll be able to eliminate conflict altogether by refusing to "close our minds." And that's true, in a way, but only because people who don't know anything have nothing to argue about.

In the words of G.K. Chesterton, "Merely having an open mind is nothing. The object of opening the mind, as of opening the mouth, is to shut it again on something solid." It's perfectly sensible to open an empty mind, you'll be able to fill it with all sorts of useful things. But if you leave it open after you've filled it, everything inside is bound to fall back out. You'll be left in the end with the empty mind you started with.

Malcom Forbes famously said "The purpose of education is to replace an empty mind with an open one." But openness and emptiness aren't mutually exclusive; an open thing can be empty almost as easily as a closed thing. And if a mind remains empty, what do we mean by saying it has been educated? The act of opening a jar is usually an absolutely necessary step if you wish to use the jar for something useful, but unless you then put something in it, you may as well have left it shut. An empty jar with a lid and an empty jar without one will both leave your toast equally bland, it's the jam you really want.

So it's filling the mind, not opening it, which needs to be the aim, and filling it will require you to choose what you believe is true. If you refuse to make a decision, ignorance is the only available alternative. And if you do affirm anything you implicitly "close your mind" to its antithesis; saying yes to something always means saying no to something else. You cannot say yes to opening the door without saying no to leaving it shut. You cannot say yes to the truth without saying no to lies. You cannot say yes to knowledge without saying no to ignorance.

And in practical terms, the result will usually be worse than having an empty mind. If you fill a cup with something, even something very good, but leave it open to the environment, and allow anyone to put anything in it that they like, whatever it was filled with in the beginning, it will probably be poison before long. And because a cup can't be full of milk and full of rusty nails at the same time, the more of the bad stuff you allow in, the less of the good stuff you'll have. Ideas work in very much the same way. You can't really have an empty mind. A person begins having beliefs well before they are even aware of what a belief is. And you can't really hold an idea and its opposite in your head at the same time. You must either affirm neither of them and be resigned to ignorance (which is usually impractical), or affirm one and implicitly deny the other.

This means that if you're trying very hard to keep your mind open no matter the cost, it will be at the expense of your ability to truly decide what to believe. Whether you consciously make the choice or not, you will never get anywhere if you believe you need to make a left turn and a right turn at the same time, or run and lie down all at once. You simply must choose, or you must stay still, and life is rarely so courteous as to allow a person to stay still for long. If you abstain from willfully and consciously making that choice, you leave it up to chance—or perhaps worse, you will have the choice made for you by someone else. There are people in this world who would relish the chance to interact with a person who isn't willing to disbelieve anything.

So while the promise of a world without conflict is enormously tempting, the price you pay is far too steep. Commitment to an idea nearly always carries a cost. There will usually be someone who disagrees with you—or perhaps even dislikes you—but making decisions is nevertheless a worthwhile investment. For one thing, ignorance usually carries a far steeper penalty than commitment. But moreover, there's also a unity on the other side of a resolved conflict that's far deeper and more meaningful than the platonic politeness of an avoided disagreement.

Even "agreeing to disagree" is better than *refusing* to disagree; it at least allows you to engage meaningfully with the person you disagreed with. Learning how to be friends with someone you don't see eye-to-eye with will do you much more good in the long run than intellectually keeping all of your acquaintances at arm's length. If you have close siblings or a spouse, that relationship has probably made the point better than I ever could in writing. You probably know very well from experience that being truly and deeply close with someone usually costs quite a few ruffled feathers, but in the end it's well worth the trouble.

To be clear, I'm not saying you should close your mind very quickly, or even very tightly. I'm not saying you should jump to conclusions, or advocating for stubborn pigheadedness. Either of those will do more to keep you from the truth than to help you find it, and they'll be far worse for your relationships, too, for the same reasons. I'm merely trying to say that decisive thinking is an enormously better vehicle to truth than thinking that refuses to commit.

So my advice to you is to open your mind only as long as it takes to put something good into it. After that, close it against the things which can't fit in without pushing the good things out. If you are ignorant (as all of us are concerning one thing or another), open your mind wide to all of the possibilities. But then weigh the possibilities against each other, and use your best judgment to sort the good from the bad. Put the good in, and close the lid. Leave the bad outside where you found it. Then see what wonderful things you can build with the worthwhile ideas you've found. You will find that good ideas are much more useful when they aren't fettered with bad ones, or mired in uncertainty.

Deciding which ideas are good and which ones are bad often involves making hard choices. You will inevitably get it wrong sometimes. You will probably find at some point that you need to smash and discard a brick that you carefully sculpted and baked because it crumbles under the weight of new information. But being occasionally wrong is simply the price you must pay in order to learn. You'll never be wrong if you avoid making hard choices, but you'll never be right either, and never being right is by far the more hopeless fate.

My truth

The next roadblock we'll attempt to deal with is rather succinctly expressed in the phrase "my truth." I'm not sure that everyone who uses the phrase means the same thing by it—especially since they often seem unconcerned by what anyone else might mean by it—but there are strings attached to the idea in every case. The most obvious thing is that it implies truth can be owned in some sense, and that ownership in turn implies some degree of authority. In the sense I usually hear the phrase used, the owner has the power, not only to decide what their truth is, in the way you would decide which clothes to wear, but to actually define their truth as its author. The implication is that you have no more right to tell me anything about "my truth" than I do to pick your favorite color.

This obviously grants the owner of the truth several advantages. The first is that they've avoided even the possibility of being told they're wrong. In effect it's similar to the perpetual open-mindedness I talked about in the last chapter, or perhaps even a consequence of it. As I mentioned, the trouble with refusing to close your mind is that in order to affirm any idea, you have to implicitly deny its antithesis. If I say "murder is bad," then whether I mean to or not, I'm "closing my mind" to the statement "murder is good." So keeping a perpetually open mind quickly reveals itself to be unlivable; you couldn't make it out your front door without deciding against leaving it locked. This means that within a community, if I affirm anything at all I run the risk of entering into a conflict by denying what someone else believes to be true.

I'm suspicious that the concept of "my truth" (as it has been presented to me, anyway) was invented as an escape hatch for precisely that situation. If I can't avoid "closing my mind," how can I avoid disagreeing with people who have come to different conclusions than I have? The attempted solution is to put each person's truth in a box. I'll build my sand castle in this square, you build yours in that one. If we privatize truth, then my unavoidable instances of "closed-mindedness" have no effect on you. So even if we can't avoid closing the mind, at least we can avoid its consequences. If we come to different conclusions, no problem, that's your truth, this is mine. No need to disagree, we're both entirely correct in our own context. If I think a sand castle should have one gate, and you think it should have two, no matter, I'll just put one gate in mine, and you can put two in yours.

The trouble is that you can only keep up the pretense that you're talking about two different contexts for so long. What happens when I build a moat that drains into your square and brings down part of your sand castle's wall? And how come your square is bigger than mine? Who gets to decide where the boundary lines are drawn, anyway? Invariably you end up in a situation where my sand castle encroaches on yours in a way that reveals we've really been on the same beach all along.

Even the most valiant attempts at privatizing truth always end up smuggling in some "shared truth" that violates the boundaries. I might say "I'll decide what's true for myself, you do the same. My truth is mine, and your truth is yours. Unless your truth is that murder is good, that one's an exception. Oh, and theft, hands off my car. Oh, and you have to drive on the right side. And keep under the speed limit…" and so on and so forth until the shared truth erodes the private truth entirely.

If truth is what correlates with reality, and we exist in the same reality (which we must in order to interact at all), then the truth is the same for both of us. In fact the very idea that truth is relative to the individual is one of those "smuggled-in" ideas —it must be true for everyone, or the whole thing breaks down. I can pretend lines in the sand truly separate us for a while, but when the tide comes in the lines will be gone and we'll both get wet.

I should clarify here, though, that in some cases, when people say "my truth" it seems what they actually mean is simply "the truth about me." And in that sense the idea of "my truth" brushes the edges of the entirely reasonable observation that it would be silly for me to disagree with you about all sorts of things you think about yourself.

I've found that one of the most inconvenient things about being a human person is that I can only ever experience anything from my own perspective. One of the symptoms of that malady is that if you tell me something about your mental experiences, I'm in no position to confirm it, and thus certainly in no position to argue with you. For example, if you say you like hamburgers, I might resist by pointing out that you said last week you didn't like them, and you ordered chicken the last time you went to a restaurant. But really you could have changed your mind, even in the second before you actually made the pronouncement, and how would I know? When the truth concerns only your own private experience, you are the authority on the subject, no one can argue with you. But the fact that no one can argue with what you say is really only incidental to the fact that no one else witnessed what happened. It isn't an indication of any authority to actually define what happened, it's simply an indication of your proximity to it.

If there were some way for someone to share your consciousness, and they were able to experience your hankering for a good burger exactly as you did, they would have every bit as much right as you would to determine whether or not you liked hamburgers in that moment. The experience is "yours" only in that it can't be directly shared with anyone else, but if what happens in your mind is real in any sense, then while it only happens *to* you, it happens *for* everyone. If your mind is a real thing, then what happened in your mind is just as real for me as the sun rising is real for both of us. There are plenty of things that are real which I haven't experienced. The fact that I haven't eaten puréed squid doesn't mean it doesn't exist, it just means I'll have to take someone else's word for whether it's as unpleasant as it sounds. In that very specific way (and probably only in that way), your thoughts are a lot like puréed squid. The fact that I haven't experienced your thoughts doesn't make them any less real.

By definition, truth correlates directly with what happens in reality. That makes defining truth inherently problematic, since there's really no way for me to affect (let alone directly define) truth at all except by affecting reality, and my powers to do so are extremely limited. There's usually very little I can do about the way things are, and there's never anything I can do about the way things were—which is usually what we're talking about. So there's some sense in saying that my own experiences are "my truth" as long as what I mean by "mine" is merely that I'm the only one who experienced what actually happened, and not that I actually defined it. But as soon as we begin referring to anything outside of ourselves, even that caged meaning of the phrase loses all relevance.

For example, it's nonsense for me to say "my truth is that the day lasts 32 hours." You can't reasonably disagree with me about my favorite color because you can't experience the fondness I feel for it, but you're just as qualified as I am to sit down with a clock and see how many hours pass between sunrises. It's completely reasonable for you to tell me I'm wrong as long as you can prove it. And by the end of that day, say we both made some error and I came up with 32 hours and you came up with 16 hours. The fact that we're both exceptionally poor mathematicians doesn't change the fact that 24 hours was the actual length of time we were trying to measure.

Where two people hold genuinely contradictory views about something, there are exactly 3 possibilities: either person A is right and B is wrong, or A is wrong and B is right, or they're both wrong. In the case of a contradiction, A and B both being right is impossible. Only a statement that correlates with what really happened can be actually true, and what happened is what happened (regardless of what I believe about it). And the opposite of what happened can't have also happened at the same time, in the same sense. We'll talk more about "half truth" later, but for now it will suffice to establish that the sky can't be blue and yellow at the same time, in the same sense. One person might see blue, and another person might see yellow, but how either person perceives it is irrelevant to the actual truth. One is right, or both are wrong. The light has the wavelength it has, and the truth doesn't concern itself with what either of them believes.

What we've been circling is the notion of "objective truth." We need to figure out our destination before we choose our direction; if truth exists primarily within us we'll need to take an entirely different route to reach it than we will if the truth is "out there." If you've disagreed with my assessment about "my truth" you may still feel as though there's such a thing as "subjective truth." It may be prudent to pause here and clarify what we mean by subjective truth, since there seems to be some haziness in the way the term is used.

Some follow Kierkegaard's approach and describe subjective truth as each person's internal understanding of the truth. I will usually refer to this internal understanding as "perception" in this book. To me, "subjective truth" is something of a misnomer in this case, since it implies that your understanding of the truth is the same sort of thing as the truth itself. But your understanding (your acceptance of an idea as true or false) is simply a mental state. And notably, you are in that mental state objectively—your mental state can be described in ways that are objectively either true or false. It is certainly true (objectively) that we all have our own private impressions of what the truth is, but that impression of the truth is as different from the truth itself as your shadow is different from your body. There wouldn't be a shadow if there weren't something to cast it, but if you switch off the lights, the shadow disappears, while the caster remains.

Others, as I mentioned earlier, go much farther and say that subjective truth is truth which finds its *definition* within the observer, and not the thing being observed. This, as far as I can tell, is the particular brand of subjective truth espoused by many users of the phrase "my truth." The idea certainly has plenty of appeal. The ability to define truth is the ability to decide what's real. That would be enough to make the idea desirable, even without the more specific added benefit of being able to avoid conflict, and by extension be completely above criticism. The idea of subjective truth is certainly alluring, but that's part of the trouble—or maybe even the whole of it. We always have to be extremely careful when dealing with what we fear may be true, but even more careful with what we hope is true. "Wishful thinking" isn't just a meaningless colloquialism, we tend to process ideas differently when we approach them with a desired outcome.

I bring up the idea of wishful thinking because for all its popularity, the idea of subjective truth doesn't hold up well to even moderate scrutiny. At the very least, you have to admit that subjective truth isn't the only truth, otherwise you end up in all sorts of impossible situations. If there is such a thing as moral truth, and that truth is subjective, then what if my moral truth doesn't line up with yours? What if, say, my moral truth was that you were under an ethical obligation to give me all of your money? You might say at that point that since moral truth is subjective, and thus relative to each individual, I'm not allowed to say what you should do, only what I should do. Fair enough, but then what if my moral truth is that theft isn't wrong for me? If my ethics are completely private, and there is no shared moral reality, then, simply put, you can't tell me I'm doing anything wrong, even where my actions affect you directly. And while I might thoroughly enjoy it if I could paint a mustache on someone who annoys me while maintaining the moral high ground, subjective morality just doesn't work. The lines in the sand are inevitably washed away at the first hint of a wave.

You could, of course, bypass that particular conundrum by saying that morality isn't actually real, subjectively or otherwise. We'll discuss that possibility in more depth later on, but if examining subjective truth through the lens of ethics doesn't suit you, examining any truth will do, really—especially any truth that pertains to more than one person, or to no one in particular. What if the length of an inch were only subjectively true? Or what if the price of bread were only subjectively true? As soon as we try to think about anything beyond ourselves, or attempt any kind of interaction with another person, we're immediately confronted with the necessity of a shared frame of reference, and, almost as quickly, we're given irrefutable evidence that such a frame of reference must exist. All it takes is marking the length of an inch on a piece of wood, or writing a number on a price tag, for us to be able to share the definition that initially only seemed to exist in the definer's head.

To help illustrate the point, it's worth noting that even if you experience sensations that are otherwise detached from reality, it's still objectively true that you experienced those sensations. The truth about those sensations doesn't lie within the sensations themselves. I don't need to experience them directly to understand them (at least in part), because the truth about them can be conveyed using the context of our shared objective reality, even though the experiences themselves can't. For example, if I'm hallucinating, I'm never really "seeing things that aren't real" strictly speaking. Or to put it more clearly, the "seeing" itself isn't any more or less real than if I'm seeing something that physically exists; my perception just isn't correlating with my environment the way it typically does.

Take the statement "I'm seeing a floating purple elephant." That statement is still objectively true, even if there is no actual purple elephant. I'm still experiencing sensations in my mind, and the experience exists objectively, even if the elephant doesn't. If you were to say "there *is* no purple elephant," that statement is true, and true for both of us, even though I can't confirm it due to my flawed perception. But if I were to say "I *see* a purple elephant," that statement is also true, and true for both of us, even though you can't confirm it because you don't share my flawed perception. The important thing (for our purposes) is that in either case the truth itself is distinct from any particular person's experience.

It's no wonder that it's difficult to separate the idea of one's perception from the idea of reality, given that our only indication that there is such a thing as reality is our perception of it; but ultimately none of us can experience more than an infinitesimal slice of reality, and therefore an infinitesimal slice of truth. This gives us another clue that our perception is different from the truth we perceive with it. I experience my perception in its totality by definition, but in my present state of being I could never hope to experience all of reality.

I experience a tiny fraction of what happens on a tiny planet within a universe that's infinitely large (for all we know). Reality is impossibly enormous, while my perception is measurably small. It's a pinhole through which I get the smallest glimpse of truth. Truth describes what is real, and what is real is so much bigger than I could ever hope to understand, let alone define. Subjective truth, if it did exist in any meaningful sense, could never be anything but a pale shadow, because subjective reality (my perception) reveals itself as a pathetically small microcosm when held up against the unimaginably large backdrop of time and space, not to mention the limitless abstract spaces we can explore in our minds. Humility is senseless if I'm the author of truth itself, but it is the only reasonable response to the hugeness of reality.

Just to be clear, I don't mean to suggest that the virtue of humility should stand above criticism, and therefore lends credibility to the idea that truth is bigger than we are. The statement "a person should be humble" needs to be supported with evidence like any other statement. What I do mean to say is the other way around; that objective truth is demonstrable, and therefore humility is reasonable. And because it's reasonable, it's also helpful.

In fact the blow dealt to the honest pursuit of truth by the loss of that humility is all but deadly. It leads us to the fatally misguided belief that the truth must not be any more complicated than what we readily and easily understand. Instead of realizing that what we're really after is a small, precious slice of an unimaginably large pie, we get the mistaken impression that we should be able to eat the whole thing in one sitting. Instead of trying to expand our minds to fit as much truth in as we can, we end up shrinking the truth to fit within whatever size our heads happen to be at the moment, and discarding whatever remains. Without a humble recognition of our own smallness in comparison to truth, we end up believing that we can use ourselves as the measuring stick.

Alongside "my truth," look at the maxims of our time: "believe in yourself," or "you're perfect just the way you are," or "just be yourself." We've become luxuriously comfortable with self-referencing. What's really dangerous about these phrases is that they hint at the truth, without quite hitting the mark. There's a degree of merit to "believing in myself," if what I mean is that I shouldn't put much stock in the words of people who mean to belittle me. As my brother is fond of saying "without confidence, you're twice defeated" (paraphrasing Marcus Garvey). There's an obvious truth there. And if what someone means by "you're perfect just the way you are" is that I don't need to change to meet another person's arbitrary standards, or to be "good enough," then while it's not quite an accurate usage of the term "perfect," that statement also alludes to a meaningful truth. And when someone says "just be yourself," if they mean to say it would be better to embrace the things that make me unique than to try and be like everyone else, I would agree wholeheartedly. But the problem is that each of these statements goes just a bit too far by suggesting that I use myself as the point of reference for what's true. They're just close enough to the truth to appear credible, but ultimately each of them is a street sign pointed in the wrong direction.

We've somehow gotten it into our heads that the truth lies within us, but what a small and narrow truth that must be to fit inside such creatures as we are. I'm not nearly big enough to be the source of truth. Reality doesn't exist in me, I exist in reality. Why would I look within myself to try and discover something bigger than I am? It's like looking under the couch to try and find my misplaced rhinoceros. It's like staring down a well while fireworks erupt all around me. If I look very closely I might see a dim reflection, but if I would only look up instead of looking in, I'd realize how dark and stale my poor excuse for truth really was.

I mentioned that the very concept of thinking is nebulous. I'll go a step further here and say that it's nearly paradoxical, in that we must think about thinking in order to do it well. That's maybe not as extraordinary as it seems at first (to me, at least), since after all doing anything well requires practice. The problem with the skill of thinking, though, is that the device we're inclined to use to measure our progress is the very device we're trying to refine. Measuring anything in a self referencing system is like trying to use a ruler to tell whether that same ruler has grown. If you're the source of truth, you've lost any frame of reference for measuring how well you think. It's doubtful you'll be able to tell if your thinking is even different, let alone better or worse. But looking beyond ourselves brings clarity into the mire. It's impossible to measure our thinking against our thinking in any meaningful way, but if we make our goal discovering a truth beyond ourselves, we suddenly find we have a solution to the riddle. Better thinking is that which leads to truth, worse thinking is that which deludes us. We can use the world around us and the ideas of others to calibrate our measurements. If we look out and around, instead of only looking within, not only are we looking where the truth generally is, but we gain perspective, and that is precisely what we need. If we make anything you might call progress without that perspective, it will only have happened by coincidence.

Half-truth

In the last chapter I said that in the case of contradicting statements, both can be false, but they can never both be true. If that seemed bold, then brace yourself, because I'm going to make a statement that's much more radical (at least to the modern reader), but I hope you'll hear me out as I try and explain what I mean. The statement is this: The truth is black and white. It is never gray.

The reason it was so important to establish the distinction between our perception and reality is so that we can make another distinction. The "gray areas" and complications that seem embedded within the concept of truth aren't in the realm of reality, they're in the realm of our perception. Put another way, the problem lies in our understanding, not in the thing we're trying to understand.

The idea that truth is so simple seems to fly madly in the face of our experience. It's important at this point to make the distinction between "simple" and "easy." I don't mean to imply in any way that the truth should be easy. A boat can be very simple—all you really need is some wood in a certain shape. Water, on a molecular level, is made up of only 3 atoms. Boats are simple, water is simple, but that's little comfort to someone trying to cross the Atlantic in a row boat. A simple thing isn't always an easy thing. But the inverse is true as well, the fact that a thing is difficult doesn't necessarily mean it's complicated.

To help illustrate what I mean, have you ever seen a small black and white checkerboard pattern from a distance? As you get farther away, the black and white squares become less and less distinct until eventually the whole thing looks like a small gray blur. Or imagine you're close to the checkerboard and someone spins it very fast. The colors of the squares haven't changed, what you're looking at is black and white, but what you see is gray. It becomes very difficult to see it with enough clarity to really understand it. Truth can be like that at times. If you look at it from too great a distance, or fail to account for its context, you're left with a statement that seems "half-true," but what you really have is more than one statement blended together in some way.

For example, let's say someone named Sally rode the bus to the park. If I were to recount her intrepid adventure with the sentence "Sally rode the bus to the beach," it might sound like I've said something "half-true." But I haven't really said something that's half-true, we're just not looking closely enough. What I've really done is said something that's true, and a separate thing that's false. There are two distinct facts to consider, 1. Sally rode the bus, and 2. Sally went to the park. When I attempted to describe what happened, I said 1. Sally rode the bus, and 2. Sally went to the beach. The first statement I made is completely true because it correlates with reality, but the second statement I made is completely false, because Sally didn't go to the beach. So in a sense, my *sentence* is "half-true," because half of it is a true statement, and the other half is a false statement, but each of the *statements* I made was either completely true, or completely false.

If you're following me so far you can probably already imagine how much more complicated these "compound statements" can get. Take a sentence like "There were forty two witnesses who saw the Frenchman climb up that tree, because a man in a parrot costume never goes unnoticed." There are at least half a dozen statements crammed into that one sentence. Some of the statements are only barely implied, such as "the climber was French," and "the climber was a man." And each one has to be untangled and verified separately if we're determined to learn how true the sentence is. We can't assume that just because one particular statement is true or false that every other statement in the sentence will share the same truth value.

And all of this is within a single sentence; I must have made thousands of statements so far in this book, for example. In a way it could be completely valid to say that this book so far has been "half-true," but only in the sense that each statement I've made could be true or false, and I've made quite a few statements. In other words, half of what I've said could be true, but nothing I've said could have been half-true.

Another way a statement might appear to be half-true is if it's vague enough to be misinterpreted. Imagine a car is blue with white stripes on the hood. If I were to say "that car is blue," most people would probably readily agree, but some might think of the statement as only partially true. Really, though, the statement is just vague enough that its specific meaning is unclear. The most technically accurate interpretation of "that car is blue" might be "that car is completely blue," in which case it's an entirely false statement, since there are parts of the car which aren't blue. The more common intent of the phrase, though, is to say "that car is *primarily* blue," which is a completely true statement since there's much more blue on the car than any other color. So I haven't made a half-true statement here either, I've just made an unclear one. Here again we need to make a careful distinction between reality and perception, or between the truth itself and the statement made about it. The statement is vague and "blurry," and it seems to blend a false statement with a true one, but the truth itself is still as plain and simple as ever. Or to put it another way the statement appears gray, but the truth it attempts to describe is still starkly white.

A noteworthy type of this problematic vagueness happens when we fail to contextualize a statement. It could be a statement like "I like cherries." When Sue, who likes cherries, makes that statement it's true, but if Joe, who doesn't like cherries, says exactly the same words, he's making a false statement. This illusion of incongruence may contribute to the concept of "my truth" we discussed earlier. Really, though, it's just a different shade of the problem with "that car is blue." While Sue and Joe both said the same words, they were actually making two completely different statements. What Sue actually said was "Sue likes cherries," while Joe actually said "Joe likes cherries," which is a separate statement altogether.

Have you ever stared at a ceiling fan while it was spinning, and tried to track one of the blades with your eyes? I can't imagine I'm the only one to have tried this; if I am, I strongly encourage you to find the nearest ceiling fan, it's more fun than it sounds. Normally when you look at a spinning fan it's a blur, but if you can move your eyes in a circle at just the right speed, the blades seem to become clear again. Really, the blades are always just as sharp and distinct as when they're motionless, but unless you participate in their context all you see is a blur. In the same way, truth is never really blurry, but if we lose track of the context of a given statement, our understanding will lack clarity.

Of course, this context tracking usually happens naturally. When Joe says "I like cherries" you never think he somehow meant that Sue likes cherries. All of this might seem like merely an exercise in splitting hairs or being pedantic, and it can certainly become that. I've intentionally used simple statements to illustrate the problem, but statements like the ones we've looked at don't usually require this level of analysis. I'm not suggesting that you should always think this specifically and precisely about every sentence you hear or read. If nothing else, it's doubtful that most of the people saying those sentences were nearly so specific or precise about how they chose to construct them.

I mentioned earlier this isn't the kind of thinking you would necessarily need to do all the time, and it certainly isn't the kind of thinking most people would want to do all the time. You don't need to carefully analyze every sentence in every conversation you have with your best friend. It's usually enough to get a sense of what someone is trying to say and not bother too much about the specific definitions of words, or how many discrete statements were squeezed into a given sentence. In fact more often than not, intuition will help you understand a person's meaning better than careful analysis. By engaging on a higher level (or at least a more "human" level) with the person you're communicating with you'll be able to make inferences that allow you to understand the point, even despite poor phrasing, or a word that doesn't quite carry the meaning they meant to convey. But training this skill—to see all the way to the bottom of an idea—is crucial to building upon the foundation we talked about earlier, because sometimes there are statements, especially ones which attempt to answer the truly important questions, which need to be dissected in order to be really understood and assessed.

For example, if someone says "Islam is evil and its followers kill innocent people," that's a very weighty statement that's layered with potential "half truths." First, it's a compound statement; 1. Islam is evil and 2. Its followers kill innocent people. Their proximity suggests a relationship, but either of those distinct statements being true isn't necessarily enough to prove the other; they need to be evaluated separately. And in the second statement, what specifically does the speaker mean? Do they mean "All of its followers kill innocent people"? That statement is demonstrably false. Do they mean "Some people who claim to follow it kill innocent people"? That statement is demonstrably true, but has entirely different implications than the former interpretation. You don't need to analyze every word anyone says, but you do need to know how to dissect a sentence when it counts. Here again it's not about thinking "critically" per se, it's about thinking carefully. It's about figuring out what was actually said, and more importantly figuring out which discrete parts are actually true, because most of the statements we make every day don't stand on their own two feet.

Usually if we're saying anything of importance we're doing it by connecting otherwise independent statements. Hopefully you'll recall from the first chapter that if any of the premises fail, the conclusion usually falls with it. Observational statements that directly address tangible reality are rationally easy. There's some scaffolding required to assume you can trust your senses, and there may be some other assumptions related to what you're using to detect or measure the object of your observation, but once those are in place, all you have to do is point to the object, or your measurements, and you've properly established your conclusion. But when we start talking about intangible things we have to build much more elaborate, and often much more delicate structures. Take the hypothetical statement from the last paragraph: "Islam is evil." So many premises need to be posited to prop up such a simple-looking statement, and few of them can be measured, observed, or verified empirically. What is a system of faith, really? Can it be evil in itself? Within that framework, what is Islam specifically? How do we define evil? Does evil even exist? Answering each of those questions requires the logical equivalent of a 10 story building built sideways over a canyon, and the statement itself stands at the end of those structures and builds another 10 stories further away from the edge. It's not that it can't be done, or that your structure won't be perfectly trustworthy if it's built well, but you had better make sure that every piece of it is solid before stepping out there. Without an understanding of what it takes to establish a statement like "Islam is evil," we end up making very weighty statements with dangerous flippancy.

And it's not enough to simply avoid making weighty statements at all, because what if Islam actually is evil? It would certainly be dangerous to remain ignorant of that fact. Or if you can disprove that Islam is evil you've opened the door to the idea that Islam is good, and that idea could benefit you and everyone else if it were true.

Before we move on, I think it's worth clarifying a few ideas that we've been discussing implicitly. What we've been talking about is commonly referred to as "the law of excluded middle," which basically states that either a statement is true or its negation (opposite) is true. In effect that leaves no room for anything in between true and false. One objection to this "law" is that it appears to fail in the case of a paradox like the statement "this statement is false." It appears as though if that statement is true, then it can't be true, but if it's false then it must be true (but it can't be, and so on). It seems like we've stumbled upon a situation where a statement is something other than true or false, but really that's only because it isn't a statement at all—at least not in any practical sense. The statement doesn't actually state anything in relation to reality, only in relation to its purely hypothetical self. Mathematically it's technically a valid proposition—by some definitions of "valid" and "proposition"—but it can't possibly correlate with reality, because it's a self-referencing loop. It's an M.C. Escher-style stairway which has its bottom at its top. You can imagine it to a degree, but it can't actually exist. For the topic at hand we're not much interested in purely theoretical mathematics.

That's not to say it's unimportant, but at the moment we're only concerned with mathematical logic insofar as it corresponds with truth, and therefore with reality. So even if you would agree with critics that the mathematical law of excluded middle is broken by that paradox, it still remains valid for our purposes.

It's also worth reiterating that this "black and white" binary nature only applies to truth at a microscopic level. People almost never say exactly one thing, and even when they do, there's almost never exactly one possible interpretation of what they said. It's important that we understand truth on a fundamental level while we lay our foundation, but it is equally important to understand that while truth is simple, people are not. By learning how to recognize discrete components of a statement and verify them independently you can avoid throwing the baby out with the bathwater, but if you try to apply the same principles you use with those discrete parts to the whole (or worse, to the speaker), you will usually have to either keep the bathwater, or throw the baby out the window along with it.

That said, given what we've discussed (and assuming I've done my job well), as we close Part 1 there are five key facts we can assert:

1.   Truth is that which corresponds with reality

2.   Reality is distinct from our perception of it; searching for truth means trying to look *through* our perception, not *at* it.

3. Any idea is either self-evident (like "I exist") or must depend on other self-evident facts for it to be known as true.

4. If we're incorrect about any of the ideas which lead up to our conclusion, we can't be sure of our conclusion (or any ideas that depend on it).

5. Every individual idea, whether it's a premise or conclusion, is either true or false; there isn't any such thing as "half-true" as applied to individual, specific statements.

If you don't agree with any of those five assertions, then I'm ashamed to say I've failed you. Most of what follows is going to take those five statements as granted.

What many people seem to miss about reasoning in general is that if two people don't agree on the foundational aspects of the point they're trying to discuss, there's no reason to expect that there's any possible way to agree on the point itself. And moreover, there's certainly no reason to think that if they do end up agreeing that they'll have gotten to the point the same way.

A good argument for anything asks you to walk with the speaker along the path to truth so you can see (and hopefully agree) that it was the best course to take. But if we don't agree on a starting point it's like two people trying to find the best way to get to London, but one person is starting in Moscow and the other in New York. If their paths do converge it will only happen once they're very close to their destination, and they're certain to disagree about every point before then. The person in Moscow will insist that west is the only reasonable direction, while it's perfectly plain to the New Yorker that only heading east will do. The New Yorker might very reasonably suggest that they should travel by boat, which will seem patently ridiculous to someone starting in Moscow.

So it's impossible for you to really walk with me from here if you're not standing where I am as we start. That isn't to say our paths can't converge later on; we may be able to meet up later and walk together from that point. In the end, you may still agree with my conclusions, but it probably won't be for most of the reasons I'm about to discuss.

So, to the unconvinced reader, I sincerely apologize if I've wasted your time, and I hope that we can find some common ground further along the path, but in fairness to the reader who is standing where I'm standing we must press on.

Part 2: Reason

If, then, therefore

In the first chapter I said if someone makes a misstep in an honest search for truth there are only two possible reasons. The first, which we discussed at length, was a flawed premise. If you assume a statement is true when it's actually false (or vice versa) you'll almost inevitably end up coming to the wrong conclusion. As difficult as it often is to discover and verify all of the premises required to support an idea, sadly I must admit that doing so only takes us halfway. While I imagine you may have forgotten there was a second reason at all since I spent so much time explaining the first one, we're going to talk about it here.

The difficulty we're going to discuss in this part of the book is that even if all of your ideas are sound, how they relate to one another is usually just as important as whether or not they're true. If you'll permit me to resurrect the building metaphor I abused earlier, it's not enough to use solid dependable bricks; how you stack them matters too.

Again, we won't be dealing much with mathematical logic directly. First because it's much more prone to paradoxes and special cases than reality itself, but it's also a much larger favor to ask you to keep turning pages if I can't make what I'm discussing interesting, and the phrase "if A, then B" is a dreadfully powerful anesthetic for most of us. It's worth mentioning in passing, though, that what we're primarily going to be employing (in a vague sense) is something called "propositional logic." Simply put it's a system of logic that focuses explicitly on facts and how they relate. It's not the only system of logic—for example, we've already dabbled somewhat in "autoepistemic logic"—but propositional logic is arguably the "purest" in the sense that it's only concerned directly with the facts, and not about the muddier waters of perception and knowledge. We'll wade a little further into those murky depths in later chapters, but for now we're only interested in the simpler, cleaner realm of truth itself.

If you dozed off during that paragraph, don't worry, I probably won't be bringing up those terms again. In fact, if you're disinterested you'll more than likely do just fine if you forget them here and now. If you call a hammer a "bangy smashy thingy" you might get some funny looks from time to time, but it won't slow you down much in practice. Knowing how to use it is the important part. So, with our bangy smashy thingies in hand, let's begin construction on this metaphorical tower I can't seem to stop rambling about.

We've been focusing so far on the foundation. At the end of the last section we laid out five assertions that make up the beginnings of a firm, reliable foundation, but so far we've been working in two dimensions. The work we did was to establish that those five assertions were all effectively self-evident, which allowed us to lay them down next to each other. But unless we're building a parking lot or the world's shallowest swimming pool, we're far from finished. Now we need to begin building vertically, and here is where self-evident facts have met the end of their usefulness. They've served us well, but they've done their job; we'll need to use other methods to reach the loftier heights of truth. Our primary vehicle of ascension lies in the pattern "if, then."

Any fact that's worth its salt has implications. Generally the fewer implications a fact has, the less useful it is. Take the fact that Saturn has eighty two moons for example. That fact probably has several fascinating implications for an astronomer, but for the rest of us it's essentially trivia. We can't infer anything useful from it, which means we've reached the end of the line on that particular train of thought. For ideas which have implications, though, there's more to the story. Once we've established that they're stable, we can begin building on top of them. The trick to building on top of anything is figuring out what it's capable of supporting. For our purposes, the trick to finding out what an idea can support is working out what the idea implies.

I've been talking about bricks, but if you think as visually as I do it's probably more helpful here to think of something like a rough stone wall. The stones with large flat surfaces are the ones we can use to form the base, but with the flat ends down we're left with an uneven, craggy surface to build our second layer upon. The work we're doing now is like finding the stones that have a ridge which fits into a groove in our base, or a dent that sits nicely on a protruding bit. Or really, unless we're doing something very creative, we're usually working the other way around. Instead of searching for stones to fit the foundation we've got, it's usually more like being handed a stone of some random shape and trying to figure out if it fits somewhere snugly or if it's going to tumble off the first chance it gets. Our usual task is to decide if the ideas presented to us can be kept as part of our mental framework, or if they need to be thrown out in favor of something else.

This business of combining ideas is rife with all the trapdoors and quicksand you might expect in a daring tale of adventure. We said in the last chapter that truth was simple, but working with it can still be infuriatingly difficult at times. Bricks and lumber are simple, but masonry and carpentry are still usually best left to professionals. The trouble is that in the case of our thinking, there aren't really any professionals to rely on. No one can do our thinking for us. If you read this book in hopes of me thinking on your behalf, first I'm honored that you would trust me with something so important, but second, I'm afraid you will be disappointed. In this book I'm trying very hard to provide you with thorough instructions and the best raw materials I'm capable of providing, but those three infernal words are still stamped in bright red on the outside of the box: "some assembly required." I can give you ideas, and show you how I've assembled them for myself, but ultimately only you can think your own thoughts.

Let me pause here and clarify that while you can't actually use someone else's understanding directly, it's often perfectly reasonable to indirectly depend on someone else's understanding—to an extent. Your reasoning could be something like "I believe this astronomer is reliable, and they say Saturn has eighty two moons, therefore I'm confident that Saturn does indeed have eighty two moons." In fact, that's exactly what I did when I chose that example earlier. I didn't spend hours staring through a telescope counting moons (I'm the scattered, distracted sort of person who would most likely lose count anyway [hence these incessant parenthetical interruptions]). But for one thing, I can't claim to understand that fact nearly as well as the astronomer who actually counted the moons, and for another thing, I'm comfortable relying on someone else's thinking only because, as I mentioned, that fact is trivial to me. If the number of Saturn's moons had any significant bearing on my health, for example, I would be far less inclined to simply take their word for it.

If a Nobel Prize-winning physicist insisted that there was an invisible floor across the top of the Grand Canyon, any sane person would still at least throw a few rocks to verify the claim before stepping over the edge, regardless of the physicist's qualifications. Sometimes truth is a game with extremely high stakes. It's unwise to trust anyone else to make certain decisions for you. At the very least you'd better double check their math.

But back to the task at hand. As it would be if we were navigating some long-forgotten dungeon, or an expanse of dangerous wilderness, even though the journey is perilous, the act of simply moving forward is still more or less intuitive. Inference is our forward step in this case, and you wouldn't have been able to make it this far in your day, let alone in this book, if you weren't capable of making inferences. "If it's hot outside, then I should skip the jacket today," so far, so easy. And it would be merely a chore if you didn't have the freedom to explore where you wished, so what we need here isn't so much a map of where we need to step, but a map of where we should avoid stepping.

The hazards we want to avoid in this perilous adventure are called "fallacies." We're going to be naming and discussing a few of the formal ones, but I'm not intending to give you an exhaustive list. Logicians wiser (and more interested) than I am have given names to dozens of fallacies, but it isn't really completely necessary to memorize these (even the few I mention) because while fallacies aren't always obvious, you can always spot them intuitively if you look closely and think carefully. Being able to name all of the fallacies someone employed in an argument is impressive, but the important thing is being able to tell if what they said was actually true.

The first fallacy we'll discuss is called "affirming the consequent" (again, forget the name if it doesn't suit you). Basically, in practice, it's something like "Joe always rides the bus when it rains, and Joe is riding the bus, so it must be raining." The rain is the cause, and the effect (consequent) is that Joe rides the bus. If you've been reading long enough that your eyes are on autopilot, that sentence may have sounded perfectly sensible to you. If you consider it carefully, though, you'll likely notice that it's logically backwards. The effect is used to prove the cause, but in this case Joe might also have ridden the bus because his bike blew a tire, or it was too hot out to go for a walk. In a nutshell, you fall into this trap when you mistakenly assume that there is only one possible cause for the state of affairs you're seeing. The cause you assumed may indeed be true, but you can't be sure it is merely by observing the effect, unless the cause you wish to assume is the only possible cause for that particular effect.

This might seem easy enough to recognize and avoid, but every time a science teacher or news anchor has stated a scientific theory as though it were a fact they have effectively committed this blunder. We'll discuss this in more detail in Part 3 when we talk about science and its relationship with truth, but for now it should suffice to say that there's a reason it's the "theory of evolution," for example. People (often ones who aren't scientists themselves) will sometimes say something like "Scientists have seen some of the bones in the ground that we'd expect to see if life evolved from nothing, therefore life evolved from nothing." Until we can rule out every other possible reason for the bones, at the end of the day we're really just guessing at how they got there. It might be a very good, very educated guess—I don't mean to say there's no such thing as a scientific theory that's reliable in practice—but stating those theories as actual facts is a surprisingly common, and sometimes critical error.

There's a second fallacy I'll mention while we're on the subject called "denying the antecedent." It's more or less the previous problem in reverse. It goes something like "Joe always rides the bus when it rains, and it isn't raining, so Joe isn't riding the bus." This train of thought ultimately makes the same error; it fails to account for the possibility that Joe might have ridden the bus because his ankle has been hurting ever since he discovered that he isn't especially competent at skiing, and he can't be bothered to walk to work today, no matter how nice the weather is. If it were raining, he would be sure to ride the bus, but as long as there are other possible reasons he might ride the bus, we can't say "if he isn't riding the bus, then it isn't raining"

Instead of "affirming the consequent" (or effect), or "denying the antecedent" (or cause), the only effective way to apply logic to a cause and its effect is by "affirming the antecedent." If the cause always produces the effect, you can assume that if the cause is true, the effect is true also. If you know that "Joe always rides the bus when it rains," then the only surefire inference you can make is that if the antecedent (the rain) is true, then the consequent (Joe riding the bus) is also true. Trying to use that relationship to prove anything else can only be done if you know for sure that Joe will never ride the bus except if it's raining.

The point here is that you have to be very careful when employing causal relationships to make inferences. Specifically, in these cases, you have to be careful about assuming that one possible cause is the only possible cause, or reversing the roles in a cause-effect relationship. But in a more general sense you also have to be careful about assuming there's any causal relationship at all. The fact that two things happen one after the other doesn't necessarily mean one causes the other (*post hoc ergo propter hoc*, for those who appreciate Latin). For example, medical scientists used to believe that foul odors caused disease —probably because they discovered that people who wandered through sewage and the like tended to become ill afterward. Now, however, they believe that bacteria are the cause of both the foul odor, and the disease. So while a rotten piece of meat does smell bad, and you will usually get sick after eating rotten meat, it doesn't necessarily follow that eating anything smelly will make you sick—and even if it did it wouldn't necessarily follow that smelly things make you sick simply by merit of being smelly things.

Another class of fallacy deals with generalizations or groups (called the "illicit major" or "illicit minor" if you're interested). It could be something like "All chocolate is delicious, and bagels are never chocolate, so bagels aren't delicious." Here again the problem is that we're assuming a link between facts that doesn't necessarily exist. In this case, we're mistakenly assuming that a fact which applies to one group can't apply to another group. If all chocolate is delicious, then a chocolate bagel would definitely be delicious, but that doesn't mean a non-chocolate bagel couldn't be delicious in some different way. You fall into this trap when you mistakenly make the leap from "I am uncertain that this thing is definitely true" to "therefore I am certain that this thing is definitely not true." Uncertainty never begets certainty by itself.

I won't bore you with examples of all the other ways we can mistakenly treat the attributes of groups; suffice it to say that if you're beginning with a generalized statement like "all chocolate is delicious," you must be careful not to lose track of what the statement actually implies. As a practical example, given only a belief like "all liberal politicians are definitely trustworthy," the only thing you can reasonably say about conservative (or un-liberal) politicians is "all conservative politicians are *not definitely* trustworthy." This is a very different statement than "all conservative politicians are *definitely not* trustworthy." Despite the subtlety of the grammatical differences, "not definitely true" isn't at all the same as "definitely not true," and you had better be sure which one actually applies.

Thus concludes our woefully incomplete survey of logical fallacies. We'll mention others as they become relevant to our discussion, but that's about as much formal study as we need at the moment. I have to assume Aristotle would be appalled, but the important thing for our purposes is that it's clear to us as we begin building up that there's a wrong way to do it, and that the wrong way isn't always obvious. We used simple statements where the flaws were fairly easy to spot in order to illustrate the point, but as with "half-truths," more complex statements can sometimes do an impressive job of burying a fallacy beneath layers of rhetoric and profound-sounding language. That's why it's so important to bear in mind the simplicity of truth at its core, and why I spent so much time trying to illustrate it. If you're able to dissect what you hear or read, and examine it carefully, you'll be able to discover which parts are true, which parts are false and, as you'll often hear in political speeches, which parts really said nothing at all. It can be tricky, and sometimes painstaking work, but even deeply buried fallacies become fairly easy to spot once you have laid a frilly sentence bare.

I said earlier that we were going to try and create a map of where we should avoid stepping, but that's overstating what we're able to do in some ways. What we can do is really more like creating some rough sketches for ourselves of what a trap might look like, so we can glance at them for reference when we encounter something we're unsure of. I talked about how refusing to commit to any idea was the virtue of adaptive

74

thinking taken to excess. Here we see the virtue of adaptive thinking in full bloom as we try and navigate wild, uncharted landscapes of thought. Part of the reason it's not as useful in practice to memorize the full list of formal fallacies as it might seem is that it might encourage you to think of that list as complete, when we humans have found all sorts of creative ways to fail miserably.

And even if you could completely cover all your bases, you've got to keep in mind the "fallacy fallacy" (no, I'm not making that up), which occurs when you assume that just because someone used a flawed argument that their conclusion is untrue. Systematic logic can be incredibly useful in the search for truth, and I encourage you to pursue it in much more depth if you found this chapter at all interesting, but it's still less like a vehicle to expedite your journey, and more like a tool in your belt. There aren't really any shortcuts, and even with the best available equipment, you're still very likely to stumble every now and then. If you're going to make it through the dark and misty quagmire to reach the shining trophy of truth, you will need to keep on your toes. No matter how well equipped you are, it will require caution, creativity and a keen eye. But then I suppose the really worthwhile adventures always do.

Missing the point

Sherlock Holmes and Dr. Watson decide to go on a camping trip. After dinner and a bottle of wine, they lay down for the night, and go to sleep.

Some hours later, Holmes awoke and nudged his faithful friend.

"Watson, look up at the sky and tell me what you see."

Watson replied, "I see millions of stars."

"What does that tell you?"

Watson pondered for a minute.

"Astronomically, it tells me that there are millions of galaxies and potentially billions of planets. Astrologically, I observe that Saturn is in Leo. Horologically, I deduce that the time is approximately a quarter past three. Theologically, I can see that God is all powerful and that we are small and insignificant. Meteorologically, I suspect that we will have a beautiful day tomorrow. What does it tell you, Holmes?"

Holmes was silent for a minute, then spoke: "Watson, you idiot. Someone has stolen our tent!"

I haven't been able to track down who actually wrote that originally, but incidentally it's apparently been declared the second funniest joke in the world by the British Association for the Advancement of Science, so naturally I'll assume it's at least the second funniest thing you've ever heard. You're welcome for that. Wherever it's from, it's a perfect illustration for what may be the easiest blunder to make in our noble and intrepid quest for truth, which is the unmistakably human act of missing the point.

If being all-knowing were a reasonable goal for us, there would be no obvious purpose for this phase in our analysis. If, however, we have established (as I hope) that truth is something we'll only know in part, the obvious question is "which part?". In the joke, Watson demonstrates an exceptional understanding of many things, but in any given context, it's sometimes very difficult to keep track of which facts are actually relevant. Here is an area where technical knowledge can almost be a hindrance if it allows you to slide into comfortable rhythms or routines, and forego active, engaged analysis. You can develop a hawk's eye for fallacy, instinctively breaking down complicated prose into cold hard facts, but all the while failing to realize that the facts you've just dissected have nothing to do with what the speaker was supposed to be talking about.

We talked about how on a microscopic level, truth is an extremely simple concept. Any specific statement is true if it correlates with reality, and false if it doesn't, so determining whether a statement accurately describes reality is all we need to worry about. If you take a step back, and begin looking at statements in the context of an argument, the ways in which statements relate to each other to support a conclusion involve a separate set of pitfalls, which we often call fallacies. As we take another step back, instead of looking at how premise relates to premise, we're looking at whether the conclusion itself is actually relevant to whatever we're trying to learn or decide.

In short, an argument can be perfectly well formed, with completely accurate premises that are appropriately related to one another, and still be utterly useless to a given discussion. Even more briefly: a perfectly good argument can still thoroughly miss the point.

An argument that misses the point is incredibly troublesome when employed by someone trying to be elusive, or cover up the fact that they're arguing for what they know to be an indefensible position. When an argument fails, instead of acknowledging the weakness of their position, they begin defending a completely different point, and if you take the bait without noticing the change of terrain it can end up looking as though the point they were initially trying to make is as strong as the one they tricked you into arguing about instead. The "straw man fallacy" works along those lines, wherein rather than disproving what you actually said, an opponent swaps in a superficially similar statement and disproves that instead.

The really difficult part about this blunder, though, is that it's often made honestly. Sometimes people "straw man" intentionally, but other times it happens through genuine misunderstanding of the opposing viewpoint. The problem, as I see it, is that humans are creatures which are generally much better poised for speaking than listening.

There's a lot of complex psychology behind it that I can't claim to fully understand, but even looking at anecdotal evidence it's obvious to most of us that we have a tendency to hear what we expect to hear instead of what was actually said.

Our minds are constantly making predictions. It allows us to catch a ball by guessing where it will be based on where it was, or avoid a traffic accident by predicting where the car will go if we pull the steering wheel a certain way. It's an incredibly useful skill that we naturally develop, but the problem is that these predictions have a tendency to bypass the conscious, rational parts of our minds.

What occasionally happens is that we predict what someone is going to say, and when they say something that seems similar to what we predicted, we immediately launch into our own tangential train of thought about the prediction and stop listening to what they are actually saying—all without realizing that the speaker never actually said what we predicted. I believe most of us will be able to think of a time when we misunderstood someone by failing to listen closely to them, or a time when we ourselves were misunderstood by someone who jumped to conclusions.

I think this happens particularly often between parents and children, or at least I find this particularly well exemplified in my own relationship with my children. When children are very young, parents have to make a habit of guessing what's going on in their heads. Even as they learn to speak, the meaning usually has to be more surmised than really understood. Because of this I can think of several times where I've had to double back on scolding my five-year-old for something, because I realized that he hadn't really lied, he'd only gotten mixed up about the meanings of words, or that he didn't actually do the thing I thought I'd caught him doing (which he'd done five times in the past week), it only looked like he had because I was expecting to see it. What it really comes down to is that I'm not yet in the habit of listening to him properly because he's only recently gotten in the habit of speaking with any sort of accuracy.

But while we have to work deliberately to get into the habit of listening to children as they begin to speak, we can much more easily fall out of the habit of listening to people when we feel we've already heard all they have to say. That's why I think most of us will find that there are entire groups of people (people of a certain political or religious affiliation, for example) that we're disinclined to really listen to. We find ourselves railing against what they've said in the past or "what they always say," instead of what a particular person is actually saying. When we do that, we will invariably end up missing the point, and thus render productive conversation impossible.

While it may be difficult in practice, though, the first frame of the question "which part of the truth should I pursue?" is still answered easily enough in practical terms. The truth that finds the point will be the truth that's relevant to the topic you happen to be discussing. As it is when evaluating premises, while the process is fraught with difficulty, at the heart of this business of avoiding irrelevance lies a simple concept; just make sure you talk about the thing you're talking about, and not something else. Or if you're the listener, in practice it basically amounts to listening carefully, and ensuring you only bring in the assumptions you need to fill in the gaps. In fact it's best to verify even those few assumptions you bring in by necessity, if you're able, by asking questions and getting clarification. It isn't usually easy, but it's simple enough at its core.

The second frame, though, is in many ways much more difficult to reason about. A discussion by its nature provides us a context, and thus provides a reasonably clear test for which truth is worth pursuing, since a discussion has a desired outcome. Both parties (ideally, at least) have entered the discussion with the intent to understand and be understood regarding a particular subject. If there are truths which further that goal, they're worth consideration. Things can begin to get hazy though as we take another step back and venture farther into the periphery of a given context. When we start looking at which facts hit the point in a more general sense, the pitfalls are a little more subtle. There is one blunder in particular that is very easy to make in most modern cultures, and will nearly always mislead a person trying to discover the truth.

We've talked about how important it is to examine the assumptions it takes to support an idea, but we've been talking in purely idealogical terms. There's a rational, factual framework that is required to support any idea, but there wouldn't be a thought without a thinker. An idea requires a mind, and, as far as we can tell, a mind requires a person. I've mentioned this already, but we need to be very careful allowing what we think of the speaker to influence how we think about what they say. I've brought up in a few places how I feel our training in "critical thinking" doesn't adequately provide us an avenue to truth. The biggest shortcoming with critical thinking (by my estimation, at least) comes into play here. The entire concept of bias is given much more emphasis than it really deserves.

If you were taught the same way I was, that last sentence may seem almost blasphemous. But we need to acknowledge that there are worlds of difference between our ability to investigate discreet facts and our ability to investigate a person. When we start looking at the person instead of looking at what they're saying, we are wandering into territory that we are desperately unqualified to navigate. When we talked about the difference between truth and perception, we noted that each person has an internal, private, abstract realm of thought which they alone can explore. I've been imploring you to carefully construct your own idealogical structures, and none of us can reasonably expect to reach the truth without doing the work ourselves. That's partially because even under ideal circumstances, inspecting someone else's work has to be done through a keyhole.

The trouble with the typical brand of critical thinking is that it asks us to try and figure out who the author is in order to frame what the author is saying. That inevitably leads us into the realm of generalization. Rarely does someone fully explain a train of thought from the bottom up. Many of us are unaware that our ideas have a bottom in the first place, but even if we are, it's inefficient to begin at the lowest levels every time someone expresses an idea. Most of us begin with some framework that we presume is shared in order to communicate efficiently. It's never really universal, but there are usually a few assumptions we can reasonably make when beginning a discussion within a given culture. We're usually able to assume, for example, that a person believes their senses are reliable, or that property rights are ethically defensible. Relying on those assumptions, though, inevitably leaves gaps in our understanding of the idealogical framework that supports an idea someone is talking about, and we have to be very careful about how we fill those gaps in.

Generalization is important, it's embedded in the way we think about nearly everything. When we're driving down the road, we don't do a careful survey of every square foot of asphalt we drive over. We assume (usually subconsciously) it has generally the same friction coefficient and durability as the last few thousand square feet of road we drove on, or even as the distant roads upon which we learned to drive. Driving seventy miles per hour down a road doesn't leave you enough time for rigorous testing. You have to make certain generalized assumptions about the road's characteristics and how your vehicle will interact with it in order to drive fast enough to justify using a vehicle in the first place. When you press the accelerator your car almost always behaves a certain way, so that assumption is more or less reliable in practice. When you steer your car, it almost always grips the road well enough to alter your vehicle's trajectory in a predictable way. But the word "almost" is the fly in the ointment here. All roads are not created equal; your vehicle might act very differently on a dirt road than it does on a paved one, for example. And even one particular type of road may have any number of potholes, or puddles, or things like "black ice" if you're particularly unfortunate. Generalizing enables you to do things you would never be able to do with specificity, but it always carries with it a margin of error.

Generalization offers you efficiency at the cost of accuracy. A tailored dress will take ten times longer to produce than its one-size-fits-most counterpart, but the generalized dress probably won't fit nearly as well. We have to be very careful when making that kind of trade. Sometimes you stand to lose everything important by choosing efficiency at the cost of accuracy. And the more complexity and variation exhibited by the object of your generalization, the more you'll have to sacrifice of one to gain the other. It will either take you a very long time to assess the object, or you'll arrive at a very inaccurate conclusion. You would be hard pressed not to notice that people are immensely complex, and even more immensely varied. You can generalize the size of a person to a degree, but generalizing the mind of a person is a fool's errand.

If all you know about a person is what you can see, you know exactly nothing about that person's mind. In fact even if you know one thing about that person's mind, you usually only know exactly that one thing. Making bulletproof inferences about what another person is thinking is rendered nearly impossible by the practically innumerable ways a person might think about any given thing. The mind of every person is a vast, abstract expanse shaped by completely unique experiences. For that reason, most of us would probably agree that it's ridiculous to think that something like a person's race gives us any reliable indication of how that person thinks. But I'll take it a step further and say that it's almost as ridiculous to think that someone's political, social or religious affiliation gives you any reliable indication of how they think.

For example, imagine I were to say "Ted is a buddhist, so when he talks about voting rights he's assuming so and so." If all I know are the two facts "Ted is a buddhist" and "Ted talks about voting rights," extrapolating anything about his assumptions requires me to drastically oversimplify Buddhism, and even more drastically oversimplify Ted. There's an incredibly wide spectrum of Buddhist belief. Some Buddhists are theists, others aren't, some view certain scriptures as canon in some sense, while others don't. But it goes much further than that because even within that incredibly wide field of what we call "Buddhist belief," Ted might subscribe to any, all, or practically none of those tenets, and still be nominally Buddhist. It's nowhere near safe to make assumptions about how Ted gets from A to B when thinking about voting rights. If we could accurately determine his "biases," then we might infer something useful from them, but in order to decide someone's biases we nearly always have to rely on our own generalizations about the thinker, which will nearly always be effectively useless.

If you're still skeptical that your intuition about other people's motives and ideas is deeply lacking, it may be more helpful to think about the weaknesses of those kinds of assumptions as they pertain to you personally. I would suppose everyone has experienced a time when they were completely misunderstood, even by a close friend or relative. How often has something you said been taken the wrong way, or how often has someone been taken aback by how you reacted to something they said or did? We even occasionally surprise ourselves by becoming angrier than we expect at something someone does, or by laughing harder than we think we should at something that catches us off guard. And that's with the benefit of firsthand insight into our own thought processes— how can we expect to fare any better when attempting to guess what's going on in someone else's mind?

Of course you will usually be hard-pressed to avoid missing the point without knowing what the point is, which means there's only so much you can learn from this book that will help you hit the point in a particular interaction. But I can say with confidence that one of the surest ways to miss the point is to get hung up on who it is you think you're listening to. Your best guesses may be helpful if you know the person you're listening to personally (well enough to truly understand where they're coming from). But even under those ideal circumstances you are dealing in uncertainties, which means you should watch your footing carefully.

The perspective problem

In what I hope you will agree is a delightful twist of irony, I believe that ultimately most of the previous chapter misses the point entirely. While I hope that discussion of the dangers of generalizing people was rife with astute and useful observations, it seems to me that our tent is still missing. The problem is that even when we can accurately determine some of a person's assumptions, their assumptions are still completely secondary to our own.

What I mean is that we're taught to try and look at the ideas a person presents from their point of view, and that would be extremely good advice except for the unfortunate fact that it isn't even remotely possible. None of us has ever seen the world except through our own two eyes. For all I know my point of view is the simplest one in existence, but I can say with confidence that it's immensely complex, and has literally taken my entire life to develop. It's silly to think that in the three minutes it takes to read an article I could come up with anything but a woefully inaccurate caricature of another person's point of view.

I can only think my own thoughts. It's an unfortunate, but inescapable reality. And since I can never hope to really understand another person's assumptions, especially in the extremely limited window through which I'm likely to interact with them, the only sensible thing for me to do is to work backwards. Since I can't generally assess someone else's foundation directly, the question isn't really whether their foundation is solid. A much more useful question is whether or not *my* foundation will support their conclusion.

I can never really let the speaker do my thinking for me, and it's silly to think I would come anywhere near truly understanding the ideas they thought about on my behalf if I did. When I'm assessing someone else's ideas, unless they've very thoroughly outlined their train of thought, or I'm able to ask them plenty of questions, it isn't enough to ask how they are supporting the idea. Instead, I have to determine what it would hypothetically take to support the idea they presented, and see if I can find a sturdy way to build up to it from my own foundation.

If your goal was to befriend the speaker (which I suppose it generally should be if you're able to speak with them), then empathy—which is to say an attempt at understanding their point of view—will certainly take you a lot farther and do both of you more good than cold, logical analysis. It will still take years, though, to really get to know someone, as I'm sure you must know from experience. After a long and meaningful relationship, a person often does reach something that at least resembles an understanding of another's point of view. But even then, we must carefully guard against faulty assumptions about what even our closest friends are thinking. It's strange how intuitively many of us avoid those assumptions toward a friend, and yet we neglect to apply the same prudence when reading an article or listening to a talk, where we have minutes rather than years to do our due diligence. In those cases we simply have no choice but to settle for understanding the ideas; understanding the person is essentially hopeless.

In that sense, another person's point of view—or rather the best guess I might make about it—becomes completely irrelevant. It stops being a question of whether or not the person is trustworthy, and becomes the question it really should have been from the start, which is whether or not what they said was true. Because if I can determine whether what they said was true, what difference does it make whether or not the person was trustworthy? If they were a liar who just uttered their first true words, those words are still much more useful than the words of a noble, honest person, who happened in this case to be sorely mistaken. The value of the truth doesn't really depend on how it comes to you. It's certainly reasonable to prefer an honest friend, but even honest people can be wrong. And while an honest person's misinformed or otherwise incorrect statements are usually less harmful than intentional lies, they aren't very likely to be more useful.

Before I continue, I should clarify that there is a certain class of statements for which an unfamiliar speaker's motivations may be worth considering. If I have no way of verifying the speaker's claims directly, sometimes trying to understand the person can give me a better indication of the truth than trying to deeply understand the statement. Take for example a company's claim that their secret formula is the best there is. Since the formula is a secret it's probably difficult to verify that claim without making a purchase, but the fact that they stand to gain from its sales reveals an obvious conflict of interest. Or if someone makes a statement about their own thoughts or mental state, like "I don't like myself very much," but they have a giant self-portrait hanging in their dining room. Obviously we can't know anything directly about their thoughts except what they tell us, but given the circumstances we might reasonably approach that statement with a degree of skepticism. It's important to keep in mind, though, that all we've really done is traded one kind of uncertainty for another. The fact that the seller has incentive to lie doesn't in any way guarantee that they did. The fact that so and so acts in a way that you'd expect a self-obsessed person to act doesn't guarantee that they are one (you may remember that's called "affirming the consequent"). If we have no way of verifying a person's claims, our best guesses about their character or ideals may provide us an answer with a somewhat lower degree of uncertainty, but the kind of certainty we can expect from even our best guesses will always be a poor substitute for real knowledge, and a poor substitute is only worth considering when what you really need isn't available.

All of this boils down to the fact that there simply aren't any viable shortcuts in this quest for truth. You have to build your own tower. You have to investigate the premises, and make your own arguments. If someone else's argument makes sense to you, then by all means, adopt it as your own. But you have to make sure the stones they used fit in your own structure securely, or it's bound to fall over the moment you try to put any real weight on it.

And on the subject of using another's arguments, so far we've been talking about how our impression of a person can only go so far in disqualifying their statements, but it's worth acknowledging that the inverse is also true. Our impressions of others are just as limited in their ability to qualify statements as they are to disqualify them. What I mean is that a person having a degree, or a title of some kind, can't ensure the truthfulness of their statements any more than their political or religious views can ensure the falsehood of their statements.

We've discussed how one person's opinion of another person's thoughts will always carry at least some degree of uncertainty. But really, that's all anyone's credentials are: one person's opinion of another person. You might say something like "but Dr. Dave passed 8 years of rigorous course work," and that does give us something resembling a measuring stick, but it still ultimately depends on the opinions of Dr. Dave's professors and examiners. All it really tells you is that someone else thought Dr. Dave knew what he needed to know to achieve an ultimately arbitrary level of competence.

I say arbitrary because the degree program itself is developed by people who came together and said "this is what you need to know to be considered competent in this field." All that really ensures, though, is that the people acquiring degrees will be as competent as the academics defining the program. How do we measure the definers' ability to decide what competence entails? By their degrees and qualifications? Professors will likely have had professors of their own who trained them in relevant skills and ideas, but you can only pass the buck so far. Eventually someone has to pay the bill, and that someone will always be a person. The certificates and honors we bestow upon each other can never be any less fallible than we ourselves are.

It's easy to overstate what I mean here—I don't mean to say that a degree is meaningless. At the very least someone who has spent a lot of time and energy studying is bound to be much better qualified than someone who hasn't. If I'm in need of a complicated surgical procedure, I'm much more inclined to trust a medical school graduate than my cousin who watches a lot of medical dramas in their spare time. I'm just trying to make it clear that even with the best possible education, the highest honors, and the most impressive credentials, a person is still a person, and that means they're entirely capable of being wrong, just like everyone else. And this shouldn't surprise us really, every controversial issue, concerning science or history, for example, has qualified professionals backing either side of the argument (or else it wouldn't be controversial, I suppose), which means at least some of those qualified professionals are wrong.

Here, too, we will inevitably find ourselves facing claims which we haven't the time or resources to verify. No one can be an expert in every field. Even Leonardo da Vinci, for all his varied and prodigious talents, was probably a second-rate plumber, or a lackluster gymnast. There will be times where our wisest course of action will be to simply "trust the experts," but when those times come we need to remain aware of what that trust really means. Being less uncertain isn't the same as being certain, and real certainty (at least to the extent we are able to reach it) will almost always require you to do much of the work yourself. Experts have been wrong about almost everything at some point in history, sometimes for millennia at a time. It would be an incredible stroke of luck to be born into the first generation of human beings who got it completely right.

Why truth?

I'll be honest: a good of many of you might just as well skip this chapter. In fact if you already believe wholeheartedly that truth is worth pursuing, I would encourage you to do so and save yourself some time. My sincere hope is that you will continue to pursue truth long after you finish this book, and if that was already your plan, then all I can offer you here are perhaps a few more reasons to do what you already intend to do. But it may be that you need more convincing that truth is worth pursuing, and anyway I believe there is enough nuance to the question "why truth?" (and more broadly to the question "why anything?") to justify a closer look.

I mentioned briefly in a long-forgotten tome known only as "the preface" that any discussion of truth needs relevance to be worth having. We also talked about the fact that reality—and thus truth—is ridiculously massive. If this undertaking truly is so enormous and so perilous, it's reasonable at some point to ask why we should bother with it at all.

We've touched on a few reasons, but I've largely taken it for granted so far that you see the value in seeking truth in the first place. If you knew anything about this book before you began reading it, and didn't see the point in pursuing truth, it's probably fair to assume you would have chosen something else to read. But for anyone who made it this far due to the unstoppable force of boredom (and an egregious lack of alternative entertainment), or for anyone lacking the motivation to continue their search, I think we have enough tools in our belt now to take a step back and examine the reasons we should be troubling ourselves with this truth business in the first place.

There are, of course, a few general answers to the question "why truth?" that immediately spring to mind for most of us. A man stumbling around in the dead of night is naturally very interested in the truth about his distance from a cliff's edge, or what creatures may be lurking in the silence. Very often the truth has an intuitive, even obvious value. But the demonstrable value of particular truths doesn't necessarily imply that all truth is valuable. And if not all truth is valuable, then only some of it is worth what it costs to discover. At that point, efficiency (perhaps even sanity) demands that we find a way to be selective.

There's a sort of haziness in most discussions about value since we often end up talking about mere preference eventually, but we can still do a little better here than "truth is good because I like it." Unless we have some objective point of reference, value is always directly related to purpose. A spoon's value is in its ability to deliver soup to your mouth. A car's value is in its ability to get you to work (or provide a thrill, or social status if you're in to that sort of thing). With rare exception, how valuable a thing is, in practical terms, depends on what you mean to use it for, and the extent to which it's up to the task.

That's why a broken car is worth so much less than a working one. In terms of mass, volume or any other empirical measurement we might employ to assess the vehicle, little or nothing has changed since before it stopped running. We have just as much glass and steel as we had when the car was new, but the second it can no longer fulfill its purpose, it immediately loses its value—except perhaps as raw materials to fix another car or build something entirely different (that is, to fulfill a different purpose).

So assuming we have no objective point of reference, if we mean to assess how valuable truth is (and hence whether it's worth pursuing), then we first need to figure out what it's for. There are two notable purposes for truth in a broad sense, which we can use to determine the value of any particular type or category of truth. These certainly aren't the only conceivable purposes for truth, but they seem to be the most universal, or at least the most universally agreeable ones.

The first purpose is the obvious one; truth can help keep you safe. If reality is the wilderness you traverse, truth is the map. No one would object to the assertion that being alive can be dangerous. The human experience is sometimes characterized more by pain than by anything else. The desire to avoid that pain is manifest in the very concept of pain itself. When your body and mind are functioning properly, pain is the alarm bell which tells you that you're enduring some form of damage. Pain may not always indicate mortal peril, but whether it's emotional or physical pain, it almost always indicates that some aspect of your life is experiencing some degree of harm. It follows, then, that if pain is worth avoiding —or in other words, if avoiding pain is valuable—then truth which helps you avoid pain is valuable by extension.

The obvious limitation for this purpose, though, is that only a small portion of the available truth seems likely to spare you pain. And moreover, a person who spends every waking moment doing nothing except trying to avoid pain seems unlikely to live an enjoyable life. If you'll admit the inverse, though, that pleasure is worth pursuing in the same sense that pain is worth avoiding, you're able to broaden the scope of truth's purpose. In particular, it gives value to truth that is merely interesting, even if it isn't otherwise useful. We've opened the door to the pursuits of the hobbyist, or the eccentric whim of the scientist or historian, or even the incessant studying of Karen the Trivia Queen. Simply put, we're restricted to fear as our motivator if avoiding pain is our only goal, but acknowledging the merits of "the pursuit of happiness" lets us strive toward fun.

This first purpose, avoiding pain and approaching pleasure, draws its strength from the value we place on our own lives. The second begins instead with the value of other lives. Truth lets us understand the shared plane of reality, and as such it uniquely enables us to build bridges between the microcosms within individual minds. It's easy to take the value of our own ideas for granted. After all, there isn't really anything that costs us less than having an idea. But I'm sure you must have encountered an idea somewhere that didn't originate in your own mind and been taken aback by its beauty or profundity. If you haven't, then either you have a much more impressive mind than my own, or you may need to read better books.

If I may take it for granted, though, that you see the value in the ideas of others, or even in the mere experience of interaction, then some of that value can be applied to truth as well because it bridges an otherwise unbridgeable gap. Reality exists below and beyond our minds, which makes it something we can share. There's a simple, awesome power in simply knowing what someone else is thinking. When I have an idea, it's inaccessible to you, which means I'm the only possible beneficiary of its effects. As soon as I use an objective reference point to convey that idea, though, and you understand it, we're able to establish a link between otherwise private, lonely worlds. In a sense you could say this secondary purpose relies on the first, in that you can use the ideas in another's mind to avoid pain or seek pleasure, but it represents an exponential magnification of that benefit. Now instead of being limited to your own abstract mental space, and whatever portion of time, space and matter you're able to observe directly, you've been granted potential access to the private universes within the minds of every other member of the human race.

Here it may be important, though, to clarify a subtle distinction between falsehood and fiction. I said that truth is the only way to bridge the gap between two minds. One might object to that by pointing out that two people's minds can almost as easily share completely fictional worlds, like you might find in a fantasy novel or superhero movie. But while the stories in those works aren't really true, they are nevertheless truly real, and can therefore be truthfully described. What I mean is that even if we're talking about imaginary concepts, we still need a real, objective point of reference in order to relate with one another. We both need to be able to refer to a scene in a movie or a sentence on a page in order to have a shared experience. Fiction can be shared, but only if the people involved are experiencing the truth about that fiction. If I watch a movie with someone, but we're both experiencing completely divergent, private impressions of what's happening on the screen, then we aren't sharing an experience at all. If either of our experiences were entirely detached from the movie itself, we've effectively seen different movies. We can share the experience only if we're both able to accurately determine what's happening in the story. So in that sense, even telling a lie can become a shared experience, but only because it's true that a lie was told. Objective truth is an inevitable prerequisite if you mean to truly bridge the gap between two minds.

You will probably have noticed the common thread in these two proposed purposes. Both effectively attempt to answer the question "what can truth do for me?" I said before I presented them that I think we can do a little better than saying "truth is good because I like it," and it may have sounded like hyperbole given my penchant for irony and sarcasm, but I think my meaning can be taken literally there. We really have done only a little better. The whole thing still basically hinges on "I like pleasure, I don't like pain." Directly or indirectly, the concept of value always hinges there, unless you have an objective reference point. You may have also noticed my habit of qualifying these statements by precluding the presence of an objective reference point. Forgive me if I've buried the lede somewhat (I only bring this up now to avoid burying it further), but I do believe there is an objective reference point. I've avoided mentioning it until now, though, because we haven't really reached a point where I should expect you to share that belief.

Before I continue, I should warn you that I am about to enter into territory that will make some readers uncomfortable. If discussing God (from the Christian point of view in particular) is something you would prefer not to do, then feel free to skip to the next chapter (or the last paragraph in this chapter), but I don't feel as though I can truly do justice to this subject without pointing out the differences between a theistic worldview and an atheistic one regarding the value of truth.

I imagine you are probably familiar with the phrase "the truth will set you free," and many readers will likely also be aware that it comes from the Christian Bible. I mentioned in the preface that I'm a Christian, which means I put a lot more stock in the Bible than anyone who isn't a Christian should be expected to. There isn't much point in diving too deeply here, because we haven't laid many of the foundational stones upon which the stone I'm discussing fits. But if you'll permit me to take it for granted for a moment that the Bible is worth anything, the concept of purpose as it relates to truth is given an entirely new dimension.

We talked about the value of truth depending on your own value, and the value of other people (or at least the value of their ideas). The Christian worldview holds that part of our purpose is to exist free of bondage, even the bondage of our own self-destructive proclivities. Truth is the means by which that purpose can be achieved, so if its value is tied up in its purpose, then the value of truth is amplified by its capacity to carry us toward freedom.

103

Without any objective purpose, our value lies only in our own self-referencing thoughts (our perception of ourselves). We like to be alive, therefore our lives are valuable to us, but we can't really pin that to any other aspect of reality. It's something of a stretch to say we have any "true" value at all in that sense. And it's especially difficult to find value in a person who isn't you, except wherein they give you pleasure or help you avoid pain. It's a grim (and dangerous) view of humanity, but not an uncommon one among cynics. But if we can establish that human beings have a real (objective) purpose, then we've found a leg to stand on.

I said there wasn't much point in diving too deeply, and I'll do my best to avoid wasting time, but we have to take just one more step back here and establish the difference between the opinions of finite creatures, and the opinions of God. A person never has the entirety of reality in clear view. So while the truth is real and definite, our view of it will always be in some sense a portion, or shadow of it. It's like that old Hindu tale of the blind men and the elephant, where one person finds the tail and thinks an elephant is like a rope, and another finds the leg and thinks it's like a tree trunk. We're only ever seeing in part, which means we're nearly incapable of getting it completely right on our own steam. If someone can see the entire elephant at once though, that person has complete, unfettered access to the truth.

And obviously the metaphor of a person who can see the entire thing still only takes you so far, because a human person is inherently a creature with limitations. If there really is such a Being as this omnipotent, omnipresent, eternal God, He can do quite a bit better than someone who can see an elephant—He's the one who invented elephants in the first place.

So our opinion of our own value only goes as far as our limits allow, but the opinions of God aren't caged by perceptual or mental limits. Simply put, the opinions of God aren't opinions at all, they're facts. If He created the entire universe and has unlimited insight into every part of it at every moment, there's no way the truth could hope to elude Him—He is its author.

That fact brings an entirely new aspect to the discussion of value, because, if you believe in the God of the Bible at least, for some reason He has an incredibly high opinion of you and me. In very literal terms, He considered us worth dying for. I imagine God's impression of value must transcend our own rough purpose-based calculus, but even if you limit it to that, who would know our purpose better than the One who decided to build us in the first place? If God Himself insists that I'm valuable, who am I to argue?

With the gust of this Divine Opinion at its back, the value of truth leaps an enormous chasm. We're no longer stuck with a hazy impression of value based ultimately on the shifting whims of a finite creature. If the value of a person is an immovable fact, then it's no longer merely about avoiding pain, it's about protecting something of true and unshakable worth. And the value of others, too, is no longer isolated in the abstract space where desires and fears dwell. Not only is the connection we can establish given more value implicitly by the added value of those we wish to connect with, but we've been given a very real reason to protect each other as well—even people who have nothing to give us in return. They are worth protecting, simply by merit of being people, and if truth helps enable that noble defense, its value can hardly be overstated.

But alas, here I've broken my own rules and made an argument that depends on several unacknowledged assumptions. Anyone who makes enough rules about how to think will end up breaking some of them before long. No matter how many boxes you set up, reality is always too big to completely fit in them. And the bigger trouble is that important ideas are rarely discovered in a sensible order. The journey to truth is almost never taken in straight lines. After you've laid the first stone, you often find the second stone you need is buried beneath the third. Answering the question "why truth?" puts us in precisely that situation.

It's intuitive in a way, though oddly paradoxical; we need to learn the truth about truth in order to figure out if truth is worth learning about in the first place. It's like buying a ticket to attend a seminar where you're going to learn if seminars are worth attending. It's inevitably a gamble at the outset of your journey. My hope is that if you're not willing to accept my position that truth is worth pursuing because God says we are creatures of incredible intrinsic worth (and I could hardly blame you at this point if you aren't), then at least you'll see enough benefit in pursuing happiness to continue on the journey. At any rate, I can confidently say that even if you come to different conclusions than I have, the more truth you know, the more likely you are to find your own purposes for it, and thus a compelling reason to pursue it. It is an extremely useful thing.

Part 3: Knowledge

The trouble with brains

Have you ever wondered if the world around you was an illusion? You wouldn't be the first. The belief that everything (and everyone) you experience is an illusion in your own mind is called solipsism, if you're interested. People have written about it extensively, which I find rather amusing, since if it's true then I have no idea who they're writing to. If you happen to be a believer in solipsism yourself, then I dearly hope you're wrong. I would be extremely annoyed to learn that I am a figment of your imagination.

I've warned you a few times that we would eventually be wandering away from the safe, solid concept of truth into the murkier, messier realm of perception. The beginning of that journey is alluded to in the question I opened this chapter with. I wouldn't have wasted my time writing this book if I truly believed you were an illusion in my own mind, but in a way solipsism misses the mark by less than some might think. We've talked in relative depth about the distinctions between reality and perception, but let me take a moment to restate the general problem as a stepping-off point for this phase of our exploration.

Reality is enormous. Even if we're limiting ourselves to a reductionist, materialist point of view (i.e., if we assume that the physical universe is all there is and ever will be), the parts of space and time we know about are massive. And all we really know for certain about its scope is that we haven't seen all of it. For all we really know, the parts of reality that we've been able to discover may still only account for an infinitesimal part of what can be called "real." We haven't even explored the entirety of our own planet. Humans are constantly discovering new species of macrobiotic life and new chemical and physical phenomena. Scientists estimate that there are 700 quintillion planets within the observable universe. It's difficult to even imagine that number, and we haven't even finished exploring one of them. And the concept of time multiplies the scale of our collective ignorance. Even within the known universe, we only know so little of what's happening at any given moment. Each of those planets, and the innumerable other bits of stuff floating around in space, contains a microscopic dance of molecules rivaling the beauty and complexity of the cosmic dance of the galaxies that contain them—almost all of which goes unobserved by humanity.

The portion and scope of reality that any one person will be able to perceive in their lifetime is laughably small by comparison, but that isn't even the limitation that makes things the most difficult for us. What makes the depths we are wandering into so murky is that even the reality we do experience is viewed through a lens that distorts and colorizes everything we see.

You can take the term "colorizes" literally as an illustration of what I mean. What our brains interpret as color is probably just a particular sensation we experience when our eyes detect certain wavelengths of electromagnetic radiation. For all any of us knows, what we experience when we see a certain color might be completely unique to each person. Since we all have those experiences within the unsharable realm of our minds, we always have to discuss things like color in relative terms. We know that the grass is the same color as the leaves on the trees, and we call that "green." But I can't actually describe it to you without referencing something outside my mind (engaging with the "shared context"). I can say "green like the grass and the trees," but it's pointless to say "green like the sensation I experience when I look at grass." In fact I've wondered sometimes if maybe we all have the same favorite color, but what I see when I look at blue is what you see when you look at red. But I digress, the important thing to note is that while our perception is "real"—in that it's true that we experienced a particular sensation—our perception itself is inherently distinct from the object we perceive.

Here we must begin to make some other distinctions between finer points. We've been talking all this time about the difference between truth and perception. The real importance of that, for our purposes, is that it allows us to clarify the distinction between truth and knowledge. If I've done my job well, then you're nearly convinced by now that there is such a thing as truth, and that, while it's vast, at its core it's simple. The reason I had to spend half a dozen chapters proving that point, though, is that the complexity and inconsistency in perception makes our interaction with reality vague and uneasy.

The trouble is that, in a sense, we never experience a thing as it really is. It's not really as simple as my hand bumping into a table, for example. As far as we can tell, what's really happening is that some atoms in what we call the table are colliding with some atoms in what I call my hand in such a way that stimulates electrical signals in neurons, which create particular electrical and chemical states in my brain, which my mind interprets as the sensation of touch. I talked in the last chapter about generalization, and how it always trades efficiency for effectiveness. The same rule applies here. When I say "my hand" I'm referring to a wide variety of cells which are shaped in a certain way and work together to perform a particular function. In order to process what's happening in an efficient, intelligible manner I have to make generalized statements. We do this constantly, and we do it by necessity, given the limits of our senses. "Person" is a generalized term which refers to something incredibly complex. Our perception of that person is a comparatively vague and hazy impression of what they really are (let alone *who* they really are).

Of the five senses, sight has the farthest reach. We can see what's happening on distant stars that we may never touch or smell, but even sight has definite limitations. If something is very small, or very far away, the best my eyes can provide is a vague impression of it. My hand appears to be a single solid thing to the naked eye, only with the aid of advanced technology can I begin to understand that it's comprised of untold billions of tiny particles which are constantly in flux. Even those "particles" defy explanation, all we have are theories. When we're seeing something, what's actually happening (as far as we can tell) is that photons, which are nearly intangible "particles" of light, are being deflected by the atoms that make up an object. Those photons then collide with atoms in our eyes, which translate certain patterns of those collisions into sensations our brains can process. To some, that probably seems like an unnecessarily technical explanation (and for most purposes it is), but I imagine a particle physicist might laugh at my sophomoric and oversimplified attempt to explain what's really going on.

All of that to say this: what people are doing when they observe reality is most often like putting something very complicated in a box, and then examining that box. We neither observe nor think with the specificity required to understand reality except in generalized terms. I don't mean to say that there's no point in doing that, though, because even a vague impression of something real will usually tell me something useful about it.

For example, if I were to see the silhouette of a thief on a closed curtain as they ransacked a room, and the police questioned me about what I saw, it would be perfectly fair to say "I saw a shadow on the curtain, I know there was someone in there." The details will certainly be obscured, but even the shadow of a real event usually tells me something about that event. The point I'm trying to make is just that we need to recognize the limits of our observational abilities. From the shape and movement of the silhouette I couldn't perhaps be completely sure that I saw a person, but it would be by far the most reasonable conclusion. It wouldn't be reasonable, however, to say that the person I saw was a 5'9" brown-eyed Irishman with a cocky smile. While our perceptual abilities have some very real strengths, we need to recognize their very real weaknesses as well. Our senses are ultimately just chemical and electrical phenomena that usually correlate in a certain way with our environments. That can only take us so far.

At this point, though, we need to make another important distinction between the brain and the mind. The five senses which we've been discussing all relate to our bodies, and most importantly, our brains. Some scientists and philosophers will tell you that the story ends there. It's worth pointing out that the scientists are well outside their area of expertise here, though, since if there is something completely intangible that we would call the "mind," it would by definition be empirically unverifiable. Science could neither prove nor disprove that the mind exists, so the question is really left to the philosopher.

Whoever receives the burden of answering the question, though, it's certainly a formidable task. How do you verify whether a thing exists if it is invisible, intangible, and otherwise empirically undetectable? It would typically be an impossible task, but we're very fortunate in this case to have a unique advantage of singular importance: first-hand experience. Simply put, we know we have a mind, because we use it to think about whether or not we have one. In essence, it's Descartes' "*cogito, ergo sum*" (I think therefore I am). Chemistry doesn't think, and electricity doesn't care, which means my mind must be composed of something else, or else it must somehow be greater than the sum of its parts. The closest we can come to explaining consciousness in purely physical terms is to suggest (as many have) that it is an illusion created by the complex neurological activity in our brains. If this is true, then our thoughts are ultimately entirely predetermined. However complex and even random they may seem, they're ultimately the result of cascading physical phenomena.

To me, though, this begs the question. If what I perceive as self-awareness is actually an illusion, what (or who) is perceiving the illusion? How could an illusion be aware of its own illusory nature? And if it is actually aware of itself in any sense, what is the difference, then, between the illusion of self-awareness and the real thing?

And even if we grant that everything I would call my mind is an illusion, why should I expect anything produced by this illusion to be actually rational, much less true? If human consciousness itself is an illusion, and by extension human rationality, why should I take seriously anything suggested by anyone, including the very premise that my mind isn't what it seems?

Some have suggested that rather than an illusion, consciousness is a real "emergent" property of sufficiently complex neurological systems, but to me this merely side-steps the issue. I at least agree that it's much more reasonable to admit that the mind isn't purely illusory, but for one thing it seems rather ad hoc to say that it "emerged" without any idea how it could have done so, and for another, you're still left without a paddle if you're relying on a non-rational cause for reason. If everything I think is ultimately the result of reasonless, random collisions of atoms, then whatever my mind is, it could only discover that fact about itself by an absurdly improbable coincidence.

If you're unconvinced that the body and mind are things of different kinds, I'll speak in more detail about the subject later on. For now we can get on as long as you're willing to accept the premise that the mind (or brain) is really thinking and reasoning, and not merely mechanically reacting to stimulus.

The unfortunate difficulty, though, is that it's still effectively impossible to rule out the possibility that my mind can't be relied upon, whether because it's merely a mirage or otherwise. The problem is that my mind is the only tool I might use to determine that my mind was unreliable (note that when I say "unreliable" I mean in the complete sense—not that it is sometimes faulty, but that it is fundamentally flawed or inadequate). It's akin to the analogy I used earlier regarding subjective truth; we have to use a ruler to measure itself. The crux of the issue is that only a reliable mind will be able to tell the difference. That leaves us with two possibilities; either our minds are reliable, and we can know that fact alongside any number of other facts, or our minds are unreliable and we can't know that fact or anything else. So while we can't completely prove that our minds are reliable, if they're unreliable, we would almost certainly never know it.

So if you're of the opinion that your mind is unreliable (again, I mean in the complete sense), then there's really nothing I could do to prove you wrong, since even if I say something true, your understanding of it might diverge from my meaning in all sorts of ways. But if your mind is unreliable, then why read this book? Why do anything? At that point, if there is such a thing as reason it's beyond your reach. If there is any meaning to anything, you won't be able to grasp it anyway. If your mind fails, then reason and meaning fail with it, at least as far as either of them concern you. But if you do happen to be of the opinion that your mind is unreliable, then why on earth would you put any stock in your own opinion?

We all find ourselves in the unfortunate position of starting our intellectual journeys alone atop a pillar. It's a fundamental leap of faith to suppose that we're capable of knowing anything, or even that there's anything out there beyond ourselves to know. But if we're not willing to make that leap, we reach the end of our journey before it begins.

There is certainly evidence that my mind can be relied upon, even if there could never be proof. There must be some plane of reality, even if my perception of it is completely wrong, because I must, in fact, exist. And while it is possible that I'm the only thing that exists, and that everything I think I'm perceiving is merely a dream, the act of learning seems practically impossible in such an environment. To me it seems very much like I know all sorts of things now that I didn't before; where could that knowledge have come from if I am all that exists? And if everything I experience is detached from reality, why do I find so much of it disagreeable? It may be possible that my mind is stuck in some kind of feedback loop, but if some subconscious part of my mind is creating this reality, why would the conscious part of my mind dislike it? Nightmares make sense if the mind has experienced fear or distaste toward something external, but they seem an oddity in an environment where one could never experience harm.

Those observations certainly fall well short of proof, though, and unfortunately they must. They seem perfectly reasonable to me, but all sorts of nonsense would probably seem reasonable if my mind itself wasn't reasonable to begin with. Accepting the statement "My mind exists and I can trust it" at the very least bends the rules we've so carefully laid out by which we might know anything with certainty. And since it is a foundational premise to every other idea I might have, in a sense I'm robbed of the opportunity of being really certain of anything. Instead of being sure about any idea, we're forced to settle for being sure enough. But we have to take this first parting with the safety and security of certainty in order to have any hope of learning anything. Personally, I take that leap without hesitation. I might be wrong in believing that my mind has access to truth, but if I am, then I'll never be right about anything else anyway.

What science can know

"No amount of experimentation can ever prove me right; a single experiment can prove me wrong."

– (Attributed to) Albert Einstein

Once we've made the leap and decided to trust our minds (and by extension our senses to some degree), empirical observation, which is the foundation of all scientific thought, becomes a viable avenue to truth. For many, that avenue is seen as the primary path to truth. For some it is seen as the only path.

It would be unwise of me to begin this chapter without clarifying something that may become obvious as I discuss the subject of science. I am not a scientist. I'm at least as familiar with the fundamental concepts as the average layman, and I will speak somewhat technically about certain ideas, but I'm certainly no chemist or physicist or cosmologist. When I speak of science in this chapter, though, and largely in the rest of this book, what I really mean to discuss isn't any particular scientific fact or theory, but rather the concept of science itself. And the concept of science isn't really a scientific thing at all.

To some, science and knowledge seem inextricably bound. In particular, what I'd like to address in this chapter is the tendency of many modern people to cite science as though it were something like an all-knowing oracle. If that were true, then science should certainly be the first thing I consult once

I've decided I can trust my mind to comprehend it, and it seems as though many of us do just that. A person might say "well, according to science, there's no reason to believe so-and-so is true" or "I think we should trust science instead of listening to Mrs. Jones." If all a person means by that is that we should tend to trust people who have studied carefully and tested their ideas over people who haven't, then I would have absolutely no qualms with their position. But it seems to me that people very often go well beyond that meaning. They often seem to suggest that a scientific statement is above reproach, simply by merit of being scientific. That, to me, is a strong indication that there's something very wrong with the way many of us think about science. Since scientific knowledge seems widely regarded by many as the only kind of knowledge there is—or at least the only kind worth knowing—it's worth taking it to task for a moment and figuring out where its boundaries truly lie.

The first part of the problem, as I see it, is that many of us treat science as somehow foundational. We've talked extensively about how important it is to begin with a solid foundation. Only a fact which doesn't depend on any other facts (an "*a priori*" fact, if you're interested in the technical term) can be used as a foundational premise. What many seem to miss is that science itself isn't among those eligible premises; it doesn't stand on its own two feet.

Science, in a nutshell, is the application of logic to observations of the natural universe. The problem is that once we've made it as far as "observations of the natural universe" we've already had to bring in several assumptions that could never be tested scientifically. Not least of these is the question we discussed in the last chapter of what the mind is and whether or not it can be relied upon.

The heart of the issue is that "scientific truth" (which enables "scientific knowledge") is merely a subset of the wider notion of truth in general. All of the important epistemological questions we've been grappling with throughout this book need to be answered before science can even begin. In a sense, you might say that science picks up where philosophy leaves off. I think it's more accurate, though, to say that science is simply philosophy applied to a very particular set of premises.

And when I say philosophy, I don't mean that in any particular academic sense; we're really just talking about thinking. Good thinking is that which leads us to truth, good scientific thinking is that which leads us to the truth about the natural universe. Scientific thought isn't any different from any other form of rational thought, except that it only ever addresses tangible subjects. All of the opportunities afforded by inference are equally applicable to scientific thought, but so are all of the limitations. An idea isn't above scrutiny simply because it happens to be a scientific idea—or even subject to a different kind of scrutiny. If any idea about truth that we've discussed in this book is valid, it applies to science just as much as it does to anything else. Any rule that applies to truth in general applies equally to the truth about the natural universe.

The second thing that seems wrong about the way many of us think about science is that we think of science as dealing exclusively in facts. Science certainly strives toward facts about the universe, but the universe is far more mysterious than many of us believe. I'll discuss that mystery and its philosophical implications in more depth later on in this book, but for now a good way to dissect this idea may be to look at the distinction between a scientific "law" and a scientific "theory."

Gravity, for example, is both a law in one sense, and a theory in another. The law of gravity basically states that objects will move a certain way in relation to each other. If unhindered, an apple will move toward the earth in a certain fashion which can be predicted. It's called the law of gravity because it has been observed in repeatable experiments with consistent results. We can be certain that there is such a thing as gravity at least as much as we can be certain of anything else about the physical world because an apple always falls, no matter how many times you drop it, and thus we call it a law. The theory of gravity, however, is much less grounded in anything resembling certainty.

There have been several gravitational theories which attempt to explain the mechanics of falling things, like Einstein's General Theory of Relativity, or String Theory. The trouble with all such theories is that they are either completely untestable, or have demonstrably missed the mark in some form or another. Some of the models proposed by these theories predict things like celestial movement with extraordinary accuracy in some cases, but all of them requiring caveats, or producing glaring failures in other cases.

For example, have you ever heard of "dark matter?" No one in their right mind would refer to Albert Einstein as anything other than a genius, but while his General Theory of Relativity predicts certain things with impeccable accuracy, our only indication that dark matter or dark energy exist is that it fails to explain certain movements of stars at a galactic scale. We have absolutely zero substantive evidence that there is such a thing as undetectable matter and energy (which must actually vastly exceed the amount of detectable matter and energy), except that they must exist in order for Einstein's theory to be true.

Again I must reiterate that I am not a scientist, but to me it seems more reasonable to assume that the theory is wrong (or at least incomplete) than to assume that some mysterious, invisible form of matter fills the universe. But even if you disagree with me about that, at the very least it must be admitted that we've gone well beyond the boundaries of what we could possibly call fact. We've wandered deep into the realm of untestable, abstract theory. Which, incidentally, is why we still refer to it as the General *Theory* of Relativity.

The trouble is that so much of modern science depends on, or even deals exclusively with mathematical models. One reason that's a problem is that even very simple things can often be approximately explained with very complicated mathematical models, and sometimes vice versa.

To those of you with a distaste for mathematics, I apologize for the next few paragraphs. Feel free to skip ahead if you're willing to concede that mathematical modeling has its limits in comprehensively describing the real world, otherwise, please bear with me as I try and explain what I mean.

As an example, let's say a frog can be observed hopping along at 1 foot per minute in what appears to be a straight line for some distance. The simplest way to model that movement would be to use a straight line (something like $y = 1$ for the mathematically inclined). But you could also use a flattened sine curve (e.g., $y = sin(100x) \times .001 + 1$) which would still predict the same motion with only the tiniest deviation, even though it's much more complicated. And the inverse is true as well, if the frog was actually moving along a curve like that, a straight line would seem to fit the bill nearly as well, even though it drastically oversimplifies what's actually happening.

Something like $y = .001tan(.1x) + 1$ is even more problematic, because from $x = 0$ to around $x = 15$, y is practically identical to a straight line, but at $x = 15.5$ the values diverge wildly (if you graph those equations, you'll see what I mean). Or something like a very shallow parabola, which near the vertex will look a lot like a straight line, but will diverge more and more the further you get from that point. If what you're trying to model actually follows $y = 1$ you'll have little or no indication that you've got the wrong model until you're outside a particular range of x values. And if that range of values comprises the entire scope wherein you're able to take measurements, there's simply no way to know you've got the wrong model. And this math is far, far simpler than almost anything a theoretical physicist might be doing. Simply put, mathematical modeling is extremely difficult to do well, and when you've done it wrong, there may be no way to know it.

Another reason that's a problem is that once you've strayed beyond those limits of observability (as much of cutting edge science has done), you have to make several important, untestable assumptions in order to assume extrapolation will work at all. The notion of "constants" is central to almost every cosmological theory we have, whether we're talking about the size of the universe, the distance and movement of faraway galaxies, or even the age of the universe. We have to assume that the force of gravity is constant, and that it's been precisely the same (relative to nearby matter) everywhere in space throughout the history of the universe. We have to assume that light will maintain its precise speed and direction (perhaps bending slightly around large objects, if Einstein was right) no matter how far it travels. In the context of the frog illustration, if you're intending to predict where the frog will be, you have to assume the frog isn't going to decide to take a sharp left turn the second you look away (as frogs often will, being generally uncooperative by nature).

But not only have we been unable to measure gravity except in relation to itself for most of human history (let alone the supposed billions of years the universe has been around), even since we began measuring it the value of the gravitational "constant" has apparently changed! And we have to assume that light will travel at exactly the same speed across entire galaxies, when we've only been able to measure how it behaves across the tiniest fraction of that distance (and incidentally we've apparently only been able to measure the speed of reflected light, which leaves open questions about how it behaves in any one particular direction). What if five thousand years ago the gravitational force was only half of what it is today in a neighboring galaxy for some unknown reason? How would we know? What if light travels faster today than it did before we started measuring it? Or what if it begins to curve or slow down after traveling a few billion kilometers? We have to make completely untestable assumptions in order to say something like "the universe is 13.8 billion years old." And yet that exact statement is consistently posited as concrete fact, when it's really a theory based on theories, based on theories. It's a very sophisticated, very complex theory, but it's critically important to keep in mind that all "very sophisticated, very complex theory" really means in practice is "particularly well educated guess."

And yet we can't seem to stop stating those educated guesses as facts, and I think in part that's due to the third problem I see with how we think of science. We treat science as though it doesn't require a worldview. Not only do we neglect its foundation, we also seem to treat it as if it existed in a vacuum, independent of any cognitive context. We act as though you won't (or at least shouldn't) think about science differently if you're a naturalist, or a theist, or a reductionist, or whatever other kind of "ist" you might care to mention. We treat scientific thought as some invariable, transcendent form of thinking. People very often seem to forget that just as thinking is always done by a thinker, science is always done by a scientist. Science itself is nothing without minds to employ its methods, and those minds will always bring assumptions into the arena. Newton's Laws of Motion might not have happened without Aquinas. Einstein's General Relativity might not have happened without Kant. Bohr's Quantum Mechanics probably wouldn't have happened without Kierkegaard.

That leads to my fourth problem with the way we think about science, which comes in two primary forms. The first form is that people treat science as though it is in direct contradiction with the idea of faith. As I said in the last chapter, even assuming that you can trust your senses at all, which is the foundation of empirical observation, is a leap of faith. But beyond that, so much of modern science has to be (and largely has been) merely accepted, without anything resembling proof. To be clear, when I use the word "faith" I don't mean to say belief in spite of evidence. No one reasonable believes something if all available evidence suggests otherwise. Faith isn't belief in spite of evidence, faith is belief in lieu of proof. Modern science constantly makes exactly that kind of leap. There is nothing resembling proof that dark matter exists, and yet research carries on, costing millions in government funding. There is nothing resembling proof that observing a particle somehow changes its state of being (there couldn't be, you can't observe it without observing it), and yet that brand of Quantum Mechanics is essentially touted as fact in universities all over the world.

The second form of the problem (which I imagine is the real reason why people often believe science requires no worldview) is the marrying of science with a naturalistic worldview. In fact, the very idea of extrapolating based on constants to explain everything in the universe seems to presume naturalism (which assumes that the natural, physical universe is all that exists).

Imagine you were standing near a desert road which stretched in a straight line from east to west as far as you could see in either direction (and for the sake of argument, try and imagine you'd never seen a road before). Now imagine you watched the first car you'd ever seen drive into and then out of sight along that road at a constant speed. Despite its apparent constancy, no one with any significant life experience would assume that car had begun an infinite distance to the east and would continue driving for an infinite distance west without ever changing its speed or course. The idea of it sounds absurd because nothing we observe in every day life is actually constant. In fact most of what we see is steadily decaying into chaos. Even those things which have an apparent regularity are constantly in flux, like the cycle between night and day, or the changing seasons. When we see something that appears constant and consistent, like the car's trajectory, we assume we witnessed the exception, not the rule. We assume that the car's journey had a beginning, and it traveled at any number of speeds in any number of different directions before it began its monotonous trek along that desert road, and that its journey might presumably take a winding course as it approaches its inevitable end.

The only thing that could make eternal physical constants seem intuitive, despite the fact that they fly in the face of the rest of our experience, is the assumption that since nothing in the physical universe that we know of is able to alter the force of gravity, it cannot be altered, and therefore has never, and will never be altered. To me it seems as though naturalism is the only worldview in which it may seem more reasonable to assume that there is such a thing as dark matter and energy, even though we haven't been able to find it after a century of searching. In naturalism (where time plus matter plus energy must equal everything) you're not allowed to consider the idea that something above nature gave the galaxies a push, so you replace a mystical force or being with mystical matter and energy. Outside of naturalism even if we assume Einstein got it completely right it might be "dark" anything, really. In either case, though, it is your worldview that fills in the gaps, not science. Science in its purest form is silent regarding the unobservable.

Thinking about natural things doesn't require that you never think about supernatural things. In fact many of the founders of modern science, like Galileo, Pascal, Pasteur and Newton were ardent theists. Even Einstein was in a sense—or at least he wasn't a naturalist. There's no significant difference in practice between trying to explain how a thing works and trying to explain how God makes a thing work. There's nothing inherently incompatible between theism (or most other forms of supernaturalism) and science, any more than there's anything incompatible between brushing your teeth and combing your hair. Saying that science precludes the possibility of the supernatural is like insisting that a vegetable garden can't exist because you found carrots in a grocery store. You could conceivably prove scientifically that something supernatural must exist, but no amount of studying nature could ever disprove the existence of the supernatural, in the same way that no amount of studying the darkest depths of the ocean could ever disprove the existence of stars. As long as a person believes that the senses can be trusted, and that reasoning is a viable vehicle to truth, it is unreasonable to insist that they cannot do scientific thinking (and do it well) purely due to their non-scientific beliefs.

All of this really boils down to a single, enormous error. When we speak of science as though it were an infinite, infallible source of information, and place it above reproach, we've elevated it to the position of a god. We may not worship it in any typical religious sense, but we've certainly put our faith in it. Some of the people we call professors and researchers might almost as aptly be described as acolytes and disciples of science for all of the unwavering devotion they show it. That devotion makes many of us all too willing to sweep its weaknesses under the rug.

But faith in science is sorely misplaced. Science is nothing. To answer the titular question of this chapter, science can know nothing. Science has no mind. It is utterly devoid of will, let alone virtue. It is every bit as lifeless as the wood and stone our ancestors idolized. A scientist can think, a scientist can discover, a scientist can create. Science can do nothing of the sort. If you're going to put your faith somewhere, a scientist is a much worthier candidate. By all means put your faith in scientists if that seems reasonable to you, but put none of it in mere science.

As for me, I'm willing to put only a carefully measured amount of faith in scientists in general. There are bad mechanics, bad lawyers, and bad teachers, it seems reasonable that there should also be quite a few bad scientists (in fact we know of quite a few of them historically). The illusion that science is a flawless paragon of wisdom may comfortably pass casual scrutiny only because we're able to speak of it as a mysterious force which is only truly understood by the elite. Most of us have spent too much time living as human beings to harbor any similar illusions about the perfection of people. And even the exceptionally proficient scientists are still ultimately people, which means they're bound to be wrong about one thing or another eventually. In fact, to me, most of science throughout all of history seems to be exceptionally brilliant people discovering how wrong the exceptionally brilliant people who came before them were. I see no reason to expect that pattern to end with my generation; at least I don't get the impression that our predecessors were any less confident in their conclusions than we are.

That isn't to say that there aren't incredibly brilliant minds practicing science; certainly many of them are much more brilliant than my own. And I think all sorts of conclusions that scientists have come to are completely reliable. I'm perfectly willing to trust the chemists and biologists who developed antibiotics and anesthesia. They've thoroughly tested their theories and established the safety of the relevant substances and procedures. I'm perfectly willing to trust the physicists who figured out how my vehicle should be assembled. Millions of those vehicles are traveling safely to their destinations even as I write this sentence, and that is an extraordinary achievement if you think about it. Even moving into the realm of theory, there are plenty of scientists with theories that seem very reasonable to me (although I try to be very careful not to confuse them with facts). If you are willing to put your faith in scientists, at the very least I think you could do much worse. Many of them seem to be extraordinarily capable, as human beings go. So by all means, put some of your faith in scientists if that seems reasonable to you, but whatever you do, for heaven's sake, do not put your faith in science.

What minds can know

There are certainly other concepts like science that we tend to deify, like tradition, or education, or progress, but I won't address them in depth as I would largely be repeating the argument I just made. A concept cannot know anything. It doesn't have the ability to discover or impart knowledge on its own. Trust your forefathers if you wish, but don't trust tradition. Trust your teachers if you wish, but don't trust education. Trust a visionary if you wish, but don't trust progress. Any real study of knowledge must be a study of minds, not merely a study of ideas. You can never assume something is true simply because it comes to you via tradition, or science, or education.

Obviously, though, knowing where knowledge *doesn't* come from can't take us very far in figuring out where it *does* come from. It's all well and good knowing that knowledge doesn't come from science or tradition themselves, but it begs the question if we intend to explain how knowledge can be acquired. We've discussed how truth exists simply because the things it describes exist. Knowledge isn't merely a facet of reality like truth, though. Truth is possible as long as even a single thing can be said to exist, but knowledge requires a very particular thing to exist; it requires a mind. But while there's certainly no hope of knowledge without a mind, it perhaps remains to be answered whether even a mind is enough.

I've gone to great lengths to separate the ideas of truth and perception, which, as I've alluded to, is because perception is the barrier that separates truth and knowledge. We reach the crux of it here. The question at hand is "how do I translate truth into knowledge?" We've addressed the edges of that question a dozen different ways so far in this book, but an understanding of the mind is needed before we have the full picture. We've spent two chapters defining the mind and addressing the limits of perception because the only chance we have of acquiring knowledge is if truth can somehow fit through the narrow, shifting window of our perception to reach our minds and become knowledge.

So now the scene is finally set. We have things which exist, and the truth, simply by merit of those things' existence, exists as well. At the other end of a bottomless chasm lies the mind. And across this chasm spans a narrow, precarious rope bridge which we call perception, swinging back and forth, looking solemn and hazardous. I've painted a nearly hopeless scene because I mean to illustrate what a nearly hopeless situation we find ourselves in. But nearly hopeless is an entirely different thing than completely hopeless. I believe that bridge can be crossed, and I believe we can use it to reach farther than many of us might expect. But I also think it's incredibly important that we realize once we've crossed what a wonder it is to have made it to the other side.

In one sense, I'm speaking to a very small minority of readers as I'm trying to prove that the bridge can be crossed. To have come this far in reading, whether you're aware of it or not, in a practical sense you have already taken it for granted that our minds can cross the gap and achieve real knowledge. I suppose in a world where knowledge is inaccessible you might just as well read a book as do anything else (although I can't imagine why you'd choose this one), but to say it was pointless would be an understatement. If it can't lead you to knowledge, there's little point in thinking at all—unless it leads you to pleasure of some kind, I suppose, but even that it could only do by coincidence without knowledge.

But there's another sense in which we're very often hesitant to cross the space between truth and knowledge, and to me it seems to betray a flaw in our thinking. Specifically, it is that nearly all of us have made the leap of faith I spoke of earlier, most of us without a hint of hesitation. We have largely taken it for granted that we can trust our minds and our senses. The strange part, though, is that we seem so very unsure of the terrain that lies at our feet once we have safely crossed the chasm. Many of us seem to think of that rickety bridge as spanning the length between our minds and the answers to the really important questions, like who we are, or why we're here —one could argue that I implied that with my illustration—but really the precarious span has already been crossed as soon as you've decided it is worth trying to answer those questions in the first place. It's true that there's an inherent dubiousness in any answer we might present to the question "is my mind reliable?", but once we have decided that our minds are reliable (and our brains to some extent), logic and reason are demonstrably reliable as well.

And yet it seems it is usually only at the point of reasoned argument that we're willing to suggest that knowledge may be beyond our grasp. It's as though someone confidently strolled across the rope bridge, without so much as a second glance at their footing, and then immediately buckled at the knees in fear upon contact with solid ground. It must be admitted that both the reliability of the mind, and therefore our subsequent ability to apply reason, might be fairly called into question, but we seem to be strangely willing to take the desperate gamble of trusting our minds, and strangely averse to doing the obviously prudent thing once we've made the leap.

It may be that many of us would shy away from the desperate gamble, too, if we felt we had any other choice. After all, we're really only risking being wrong. And while being wrong can be very dangerous indeed, you have little hope of being right about anything anyway if the dice don't roll toward our minds being trustworthy. So perhaps it isn't really much of a choice, and therefore isn't really a gamble at all. It isn't so much confidence in the trustworthiness of our minds as it is a defeated resignation to the better of two undesirable options. And for some that may be the whole story, but for most of us it seems there must be more to it.

Complete confidence in reason makes sense if you've decided to trust your mind. After all, there can be no such thing as a reasonable argument against reason—it would be like using a pen to write an essay about the nonexistence of pens. And if you've decided against trusting your mind, a complete lack of confidence in reason, while perhaps unlivable, is at least sensible (to the degree that "sensibility" has any meaning in that context). The problem is apparent, though, in how selective our confidence tends to be. Either end of the spectrum can be justified easily; it is much harder to justify landing anywhere in the middle.

What I mean is that so many of us tend to be utterly confident in our knowledge of one truth or another, and yet so quick to think of certain other truths (of the same kind as the first) as unknowable. A person may cry out in outrage over an injustice happening halfway around the world, and yet in the next moment insist that ethics are merely cultural constructs. If ethics are merely a nebulous byproduct of social interaction which can't be reasoned about objectively, how can you decry the actions of someone from another culture? This phenomenon can even happen within a single thought. A person might think, as I've heard it said before, that no one can really know anything about God. But that statement itself would be a fact about God. Why is that particular fact about God accessible by reasoning while all others are beyond our grasp? It's all well and good if your standard for apples is different than your standard for oranges, but a double standard for a single kind of thing is always an error in thinking.

I said earlier (and I'll likely say again) that we need to be very careful thinking about what we fear may be true, and what we hope may be true. To me that seems very often to be the trouble here. Most of us know intuitively that there's something somehow flawed about our minds. Everyone who has ever been alone in the dark has fallen for its tricks a time or two. Everyone knows what it's like to experience a moment of confusion, or a lapse in judgment. Everyone knows, without needing to be told, that our minds are imperfect. That knowledge plays powerfully on both our fears and our hopes. It can be terrifying to think that there are important truths which lie beyond our grasp. That fear makes it seem much more likely to be true. Inversely, it can be incredibly tempting to avoid controversial, or otherwise inconvenient truths by convincing oneself that the truth of the matter simply cannot be known. That desire makes it seem much more likely to be true.

That clearly isn't the entire answer, though. While paranoia and wishful thinking may convince us that certain knowable things are unknowable, the fact is there really must be a limit to the things our minds can know. To be imperfect is to be inherently limited. While it is often impossible to know which things are unknowable, we can be very sure that that a human being will only ever grasp the truth in part. In fact I put a good deal of effort into establishing how narrow the scope of truth is that we'll be able to access within the span of a single human life on earth. Some of those truths are inaccessible in a tangible sense. We simply cannot see that which lies beyond our vision, and we simply cannot touch that which lies beyond our grasp. And here we must address that even if we are willing to place complete confidence in reason itself, we may still fail to grasp an idea almost as easily as we may fail to grasp an object.

Experiencing difficulty in understanding is an integral part of the human experience. I have no doubt that even readers who are far cleverer than I am will remember some time in their life when they had difficulty understanding. Perhaps for the cleverest, for whom all of physics and history and calculus are merely a moderately interesting way to pass the time, it may be somewhat more difficult to remember a time when you've struggled to understand something (although if you're that clever, you may already have guessed where I'm heading). But even if you can't think of a *thing* you've struggled to understand, surely you'll be able to think of a person. Everyone who has lived among other people for a significant amount of time will have experienced a time where they couldn't understand why a person acted the way they did, or said something that didn't make sense.

That could be for one of two reasons. The first reason is the obvious one. You may have merely been confused in your own mind about what they did. Perhaps you approached the situation with a faulty assumption, for example. The second possibility is that you couldn't understand them because they were something which humans are uniquely equipped to be: unreasonable. A mountain, or the sky, or a tree may be complicated, or perhaps inconvenient, but it will never be unreasonable. We may fail to understand a mind in a way that we will never fail to understand a rock or the ocean, and we can hardly be blamed for it. Nature may produce all sorts of curiosities and oddities, but nonsense isn't among them.

If we're willing to believe that our minds are reliable, and that our senses relate (mostly) reliably to our surroundings, it might be fair to assume that the truth about everything in the material universe can be known. I think we often overstate our current understanding of things like matter and energy, but there's an inherent simplicity to mindless things. Even when mindless things are in flux they must be driven either by a mind outside of themselves, or by something constant (perhaps indirectly), and constancy is usually simple. Mindless things cannot choose to act against their nature; they are what they are, and thus they do what they do. No matter how chaotic the outworking of a mindless thing's nature might be, it must be simply and plainly cause and effect. So if you wish to understand things like matter and energy, it may be enough to simply understand what and how. With minds, though, we introduce the possibility of a reasoned choice. Reality takes on an entirely new dimension.

You might think of "what" and "how" as length and width. We increase the area of our understanding by learning what and how, but when we begin to ask why, we add a previously inaccessible depth to our questions. And to answer those questions it isn't enough to simply continue further along the axes accessible by mere observation. No amount of lengthening or widening a square can turn it into a cube. You have to add depth. In the same way no amount of discovering what or how can tell us anything about why. We have to think deeper.

The question we're trying to answer in this chapter is what a mind can know. If we're willing to begin with the assumption that our perception does in fact provide us a means of connecting with reality, then there's no reason to disbelieve what has been proven by observation; we can confidently call it knowledge. The trees which I see outside my window as I write this exist. They may not be exactly what they seem to be, but I can see them, I can touch them. I can know what they are (to some degree of precision), and I can know how they are, which is to say I can know that they're plants of a certain kind which came from a seed, which will grow and eventually die. But to know why they are is an altogether different kind of question. If all I can do is see and touch the trees themselves, I will never know why they exist. The answer doesn't lie along the "what" axis, nor the "how"; it is in a completely different direction. And if you find yourself moving in the wrong direction, it doesn't matter how far you travel, you will never reach your destination.

Before I continue I must make a distinction in what I mean when I say "why." An evolutionary biologist, for example, might think it foolish of me to say that I can't know why a tree exists by examining it closely. They might suggest that the reason the tree exists outside my window is that plants reproduced over and over to produce via natural selection this particular plant with its particular traits which are well suited to the climate I live in. And in colloquial English we might say that's a reasonable explanation of why the tree exists as it does, but in the sense that I mean, all we've really done is attempt to explain *how* the tree came to exist as it does, and not actually *why*. When someone asks "why" in English, they may be trying to ascertain one of two things: either the direct cause of the state of being they observe, or the actual purpose for it. We use the same word, but these are questions of entirely different kinds. If I were to ask "why is the sky blue," one might respond "because the atmosphere scatters different wavelengths of light in a particular way." The answer really tells us about how refraction and diffusion work. But if we were to ask a painter why the sky in her painting was blue, you would expect a response like "Because it was a very bright and beautiful day, and I wanted to capture it on this canvas." The former is merely a description of how things are, the latter describes a genuine, deliberate purpose.

Real purpose must always be deliberate. There are theorists who say that everything we see around us, even life itself, is merely a product of blind, random chance. Explaining the mind in this way begs too many questions for my tastes, but even if we concede that the entire physical universe could have simply come to be—that order could have somehow been derived as a natural byproduct of chaos—it still cannot have produced genuine meaning. I discussed at length how truth is always equally an acceptance of an affirmative idea, and a rejection of all contradictory ideas. Purpose shares this characteristic. A real purpose requires a desire. A real purpose requires that someone decided the way a thing should be, and, in doing so, rejected all other ways it could have been.

So we find ourselves at the fork in the road that I've warned you about. We cannot build up without laying the foundation, and here we reach an impasse. We've beaten as far around the bush as we're able, but now we must answer a fundamental question.

What follows in the next few chapters will make many readers uncomfortable. I'm going to talk about purpose, and that cannot be done in any complete sense without at least attempting to answer the deepest questions within every human heart. What I absolutely do not want is for anyone to feel as though they have been tricked or coerced into having this discussion. This book is not about God, except in the way that Moby Dick is about a boat, or Homer's Iliad is about a sword. If you do not wish to hear what I think about the deepest foundations of truth, please feel free to skip ahead to the last chapter. If you do wish to hear what I think about the deepest foundations of truth, I cannot explain it without discussing whether or not reality is an accident. I will not be offended to hear that I wrote the next three chapters in vain; much of it has already been said in better ways by wiser men. I have already said nearly everything important that I hoped to convey in this book. My hope was to provide you with tools to uncover the truth. What comes next is simply an example of how to apply those tools in the context of a deeply important question.

That question, as I have said, is one of purpose. Our hypothetical painter can tell us why the sky in the painting is blue because a painter can do something that no mindless thing can do; she can decide. It's sensible to ask the painter why the sky is blue, it's pointless to ask the painting. There are all sorts of ways we might be able to determine the direct cause of a painting's appearance, things like pigments and the behavior of light, but that doesn't answer the question of genuine purpose. Meaning is an idea, and an idea can exist only in a mind. Without meaning there can be no purpose. Without a mind there can be no meaning. If there were a painting with no painter, if the colors fell where they fell by chance, or blind deterministic processes, you might recognize an apparent order, but it would be an illusion. You might see what seemed to be a correspondence in the image to some picturesque landscape, but it would be merely a coincidence. You might very reasonably call it beautiful, but you couldn't call it meaningful.

We've been trying to determine what a mind can know. For this new dimension, this question of purpose, we first need to determine if indeed there is anything to know in the first place. It's simple enough to determine whether there is a what and a how to be known. Whatever the universe is, you and I must exist in it, and if our minds can be trusted, then at least some of it can be known. But to answer a question of purpose, it isn't enough to look at the universe, we must look through and beyond it. It isn't enough to see, we must perceive.

Did someone paint the sky?

This, by my estimation, is the single most important question a person could ask. That is why it is the question I have chosen to demonstrate and apply everything we have examined so far. No other answer could have such profound implications. Is there a reason that the sky looks the way it does, or is that simply the way it happens to be?

Is the practically incomparable beauty splashed across the entire horizon at sunset merely a coincidence? And if we were the product of blind chance ourselves, is it still another wondrous coincidence that we happened to be not only creatures which can think, but ones that can appreciate the sunset's beauty? Is it sheer dumb luck that no one anywhere on this planet must wait more than a single day to see that beauty, refreshed and renewed in a completely unique way? Are the brilliant purples and oranges, or dark and tumultuous displays of breathtaking power, mere accidents?

If it is merely a coincidence, it's an incredibly fortunate one, but if it isn't a coincidence then it's much more than fortunate, it's meaningful. And moreover it's meaningful in a way that is otherwise impossible, because a sky can't decide to be beautiful. As far as anyone can tell, the sky doesn't know how it will be perceived, and if it did, I suspect it wouldn't care. But if a cosmic Painter decided that the sky should be beautiful for your sake, then every time we see a sunset, we get a glimpse beyond the facade. We step inside the painting. Now we begin to move from the prose of length and width, into the poetry of depth. Depth is apt as a metaphor, for now we dive. We will grapple with the question at the heart of all other questions. Limited as my own wisdom may be, I've prepared you as well as I'm able, and I hope I've done well. Hold fast, friend, and muster your wits, for we stand now at the cusp of the greatest trial your mind is likely to face. "Courage, dear heart."

Part 4: Wisdom

In the beginning

"God is dead." Or so says Nietzsche's "madman."

It's powerful-sounding rhetoric to be sure, but of course dead is one thing God could never be. If God never existed, which is what Nietzsche really believed when he wrote those words, then He can't have died. And if He did exist, and then died (against His will), then by definition He was never really God to begin with.

Of course what Nietzsche really meant was that the idea of God was dead, because that's all Nietzsche thought God was. But if he was right about God being merely an idea, it would seem that the idea is nearly as immortal as the genuine article. Nietzsche seemed to have been under the impression that the final word about God had been spoken. Certainly there are those today who agree with him, but they remain in the minority despite Nietzsche's bold proclamation over a century ago. We seem far too quick to ring the death bell for ideologies. Hawking said philosophy was dead, Nietzsche said God was dead, and yet now Hawking and Nietzsche are both dead, and here I am still philosophizing about God. Whether there is such a thing as God or not, the idea doesn't seem to be going anywhere any time soon.

The idea of God isn't really where we begin, though. I don't intend to begin with a hypothesis in the typical sense. If you want to build something sturdy it's generally better to keep your eyes primarily on the bricks you're laying than to keep your eyes fixed on where you hope you'll be able to build up to (or worse, where you're afraid you might end up). That is to say if you want to find the truth, you will be much more likely to succeed if you look for the truth itself, and not for what you think the truth is. In fact, I'm only mentioning the Judeo-Christian God explicitly here to avoid anyone feeling as though they've had the rug pulled out from under them when I state later on that I believe that's where the evidence leads, and to provide some context to the discussion. Instead of trying to prove or disprove the idea of God directly, we will begin with a few very simple observations, and examine whether or not something "God-like" is necessary to explain them (or at least more probable than the available alternatives). We won't be trying to prove a specific point, so much as trying to find the best answer to several exceptionally important questions. We will begin at the bottom and try to build up.

There are a few things that are worth identifying before diving too deeply. If God does exist, He clearly doesn't wish to make Himself completely obvious to every person at every time. Regardless of why that is, we have to begin with the assumption that we're talking about a God that is nevertheless detectable in some way (perhaps indirectly). If we aren't, then it's a hopeless case. If there is such a thing as a god which is completely beyond our intellectual reach, we'll never be able to find any evidence that it does or doesn't exist. It's a vaguely interesting thought exercise, but otherwise a pointless discussion.

Another thing that's worth clarifying at the outset is something I discussed briefly while addressing the idea of science. Many modern people seem to be under the impression that faith and reason somehow stand at odds. I want to make it clear that it wasn't an accident that I've spent so much time and energy discussing what truth is and how we can use reason to discover it. I certainly wouldn't ask you to dispense with reason now.

It must be assumed at the outset that God's existence isn't completely undeniable, since there are clearly a large number of people who do indeed deny it. I suppose a person can deny just about anything with proper motivation, but the heat of the controversy strongly suggests that there is a gap between where the evidence ends and affirming God begins. When I speak of faith (and I won't speak of it often in this book) I'm speaking merely of what fills that gap—and I think many will be surprised at just how small that gap is. I'm not asking you to deny what you know to be reasonable, I'm only asking you, in lieu of concrete proof, to prefer the most reasonable explanation.

Whether that kind of faith sounds agreeable to you or not, it's simply no use trying to avoid it. You need that kind of faith to think about nearly anything. Since it's impossible to really verify whether you can trust your mind, everything you believe carries with it at least a small degree of uncertainty. It can't be proven that other people exist—that they're more than figments of your imagination. It's simply the most reasonable conclusion. It can't be proven that your friends or family love you, it's simply the most reasonable conclusion. There are all sorts of things which can't be proven, but which we accept on faith, often without a second thought. You can't be completely sure of your conclusion, but it's beyond a "reasonable doubt."

If you really employ the careful thinking we've spent so much time discussing, you will find you can rarely be completely sure about anything—but that isn't to say you can't be sure enough. When reasoning, you take the leap in trusting your mind to begin with. Reason begins with faith, and faith begins again where reason ends; at no point do they contradict one another. They are complimentary by nature.

With all of that said, I'll be taking it for granted from here on out that your mind is a viable tool for discovering and understanding truth. As I mentioned, rather than beginning with an idea and trying to build up to it directly, we're going to begin with a few simple observations, and follow them where they lead.

The first thing we'll be observing with our minds is that we have minds with which to observe. I won't rehash everything we already discussed when we explored what a mind is, but it's worth reiterating a few things. For one thing, some believe that the mind is merely an illusion. To me, self-awareness lays that theory to rest. An illusion that was aware of its own illusory quality would be no different from a real mind. Call it what you will, but it's difficult to deny that there's something about a mind which makes it utterly unique in nature.

Consciousness is the quality of the mind which throws the proverbial wrench in the naturalistic works. It is an entirely different kind of thing from anything we observe. We see all sorts of examples in nature of how two things can combine to produce something different from the original materials, but never something of a completely different kind. Animals beget animals, plants beget plants, streams beget lakes, extraterrestrials beget platypuses (I assume), and so on. Even in the extreme cases, different kinds of matter and energy can be combined to produce matter and energy with different properties than the components you started with, but the products will always be matter and energy. In nature, what we see is always, in the strictest sense, the sum of its parts. Energy can never be created or destroyed (by natural processes, at least) it can only be converted into a different kind of energy. The same is true of matter. There are some scientists who believe matter can be converted into energy, but the scales must still balance. That is, the amount of energy you have at the end of the process will still be exactly proportionate to the amount of matter you had at the start.

We don't know of any way to completely destroy something. We haven't discovered any way to take something from existence into nonexistence. The inverse is true as well, there is no known natural process wherein a thing which didn't exist can begin to exist. If we assume naturalism, this seems to suggest that whatever stuff the mind is made of must predate the mind itself, but the mind, as far as we can tell, is immaterial. From whence, then, comes the mind? If we treat the mind as being like the natural things we observe, the recipe seems to call for an immaterial material.

Whatever minds are made up of, it certainly isn't matter and energy. In fact minds seem to follow a completely different set of rules. Biologists have identified in broad strokes how cells organize matter and energy to build a body, and the mind seems to grow (and die) with it, but experience tells us there's some inherent separation between the two. The most stark example of this can be seen in how differently they interact with time.

Your body must be nourished regularly. You must eat a certain amount during a certain period of time, or your body will die. Your body requires that you spend a certain portion of the day sleeping in order to function properly. There's no cheating this process; your body is completely bound by time, just like any other piece of matter. Your mind, on the other hand, seems to be much less firmly attached. I think everyone has felt at some point that time was going faster or slower than it usually does. You can fall asleep and experience hours passing in what seems like a moment, or have a dream which seems to have lasted hours, and wake up to find you only dozed off for a few minutes. Waiting for a loved one to come visit seems to take ages, but then the time you spend with them seems to pass far too quickly.

The mind seems to occupy an entirely different kind of space than the body as well. We often say that the mind "wanders," but of course we mean something different by this than when we say a body wanders. When the mind wanders it doesn't simply drift to a different physical space. In fact this sort of wandering is usually detached from physical space (and often time) altogether.

Some of you at this point may be thinking that I've spent too much time talking about the things which separate the mind from the body, and not enough about what it is that joins them, which I mentioned only in passing (parenthetically, no less). No one—or at least no one I've heard of—has any memories of what happened before they were born. In fact no one I know of even remembers anything of their first year on earth. You'll hear of some who speak of remembering other lifetimes, but even then it's never the earliest moments, and never the moments between lifetimes. It's also, of course, tragically difficult to communicate with a person whose body is no longer capable of conveying a message.

If we're trying to explain where a mind comes from (or where it goes for that matter), this puts us in a particularly disadvantageous position. Memory is the crux of the issue here. There's little point in knowing something if you can't recall it later on. But it's worth pointing out that this is strictly a condition of a mind bound by a body—or at least a mind bound by time.

Some have postulated that if God existed primarily outside of time, He would likely be able to "see" the past and the future just as easily as we see the present. In that context, memory is meaningless. You wouldn't need to keep a record of individual moments and "replay" them sequentially, you could simply "look" into the past. What if a mind like that, which existed primarily beyond time, entered time? Beyond time, that mind might have all sorts of knowledge, but it wouldn't be in the same sense that we've been speaking of, since naturally if there's no past, there would be no need for memory. That mind, upon entering time, would likely appear to us to be devoid of the kind of knowledge we're used to, and would gradually "grow" in knowledge as it gathered memories, just as you and I have experienced.

So for all we know our minds may "predate" our bodies, and there's no direct way of knowing whether or not they continue their existence "after" (or perhaps I should say "apart from") our bodies when we die. During the only life you and I have any direct understanding of, our minds are only given access to an infinitesimally narrow slice of reality which we call the present. We compile those slices as memories to expand the scope of our perception, but, at least as far as our experience as living breathing human beings goes, knowledge still has to fit in the temporal box between our natural birth and death, including knowledge about our minds themselves. Thus, the evidence is insufficient. The only thing we can say with anything resembling certainty is that whatever minds are made up of, it is not like anything else we can observe.

Descartes' "I think therefore I am" really is the primary observation. Even if it isn't the first thing that a person notices, it's the thing which enables them to notice everything else. We are thinking creatures. We are innately curious, even about our own origins. We don't have to teach children to be inquisitive, to be human is to wonder "why?" But search as we might—and we've certainly done plenty of searching—we haven't been able to find anything in nature that can really explain how the mind came to be.

Some have suggested that our intelligence is simply the product of a progression, of a natural evolution toward intelligence. The problem with this explanation is that such a progression can't necessarily be extrapolated infinitely in either direction. It may be reasonable to say that a chimpanzee is like a dog, only a little more intelligent, and that similarly a human being is simply the next leap, or the next link in the chain. That seems very sensible at a glance. One can easily imagine how a smarter dog might behave more like a chimpanzee, and how a smarter chimpanzee might approximately resemble a human. The trouble is that it's a dead end road with no sign at the start to warn you. Extrapolated backward the progression seems at least somewhat feasible until you inevitably reach a point where you've reduced thinking, feeling life down to something like a single cell with only the faintest shadow of what we might call a mind (maybe some kind of basic survival instinct, for example). But what came before that?

The trouble is that the distance from a single piece of information to an infinite amount of information is dwarfed by the gap you must cross to get from no information to that first piece of information. Getting from basic intelligence to supreme intelligence is at least conceivable as a product of natural processes, even if the odds seem stacked against it. If there is something in nature, though, which having no will of its own can produce genuine information (which is to say a meaningful set of data, something like DNA) we've certainly never seen anything like it before. By stretching the imagination, one can just see how you might get from a survival instinct to a cave painting, but getting from rocks and gasses and energy aimlessly drifting through space to even the simplest single cell, with its encoded information and capacity to self-replicate, borders on the inconceivable.

There are all sorts of physical challenges involved in getting from lifelessness to life (I highly recommend Dr. James Tour's 2019 lecture on the subject for anyone interested in the scientific problem). If it did happen, we're certainly nowhere near figuring out how—our best guesses to date have proven to be woefully inadequate answers to the question. But even if we had any plausible theories about how it happened chemically, this problem of information compounds the challenge dramatically. Not only do we need to explain how nucleotides hook together without enzymes, we need to explain how they joined together in such a way that they contained actual, actionable information.

And not only did the information need to be encoded by random chance, an interpreter for that information needed to be simultaneously assembled at random. A book containing Homer's Odyssey would still count as information if it simply sprang into existence on a lonely hill, but nothing would become of it if no one could read it. It would simply decay into a chaotic mess of rotting paper if there were no one around to preserve it. The question of how we move from no life to even the simplest conceivable form of life has no satisfying naturalistic answer. The honest answer to the scientific question is "we haven't got a clue." From a naturalistic perspective, the honest answer to the philosophical question of how the first mind came to be is precisely the same.

I hope I have made sense so far, but even if I have, we have to be very careful here. To jump from "we can't explain life as we know it" to "God created life" is certainly a leap. To make that leap is known as the "argument from ignorance" fallacy.

Uncertainty can never beget certainty. Being unsure of one thing will never make you sure of something else, by itself. I hope you'll remember from the first few chapters that a questionable premise may very well be a crumbling brick in your foundation. It would be unwise to put much weight on it. In this context, such an argument from ignorance is often referred to as the "god of the gaps," wherein a person uses God to fill in the gaps in their understanding. As we discover and learn, those gaps will progressively get smaller and smaller, and the god of the gaps will shrink along with them, until it disappears altogether.

I'm not advocating for that kind of thinking. A god which is destined to shrink until it disappears hardly seems worth your time, anyway. I don't think it's unreasonable at this point, in lieu of evidence one way or another, to prefer the explanation that intuitively seems more likely. For one person that may be some undiscovered physical process, for another that may be a supernatural being which is capable of "breaking the rules" and doing something which is otherwise impossible. But we haven't gone as far as determining rationally which is more likely yet, and no amount of harping on about the things we don't know will bring us to any meaningful knowledge.

The important thing to establish here is simply this: something happened which, as far as we can tell, is impossible. Things exist which we can't explain—in fact we ourselves are among those things. We know we have bodies, but we haven't been able to figure out where they came from. We know we have minds, and those are even harder to explain. So either we have misunderstood something of fundamental importance about nature, or we have to concede that there is something which transcends nature as we know it. There's no real indication yet, though, whether explaining the process is the task of discovering some unique natural phenomenon, or if it's mapping the fingerprint of a divine being. All of this gives us more questions than answers—but then of course knowing the right questions to ask is nearly always a prerequisite of getting the right answers.

The heavens and the earth

The natural place to begin a search for truth from the human perspective is the question "why am I here?" It's a question that nearly all of us have asked in some form or another, but the answer, for most of us at least, isn't obvious. The specific meaning of the term "why" is important here as well, as there are really two questions intertwined, which are both worth answering. The first, and the more challenging is "what is my purpose?" We don't find any satisfying answers to that question until farther down the road, so for now we'll deal primarily with the second frame, which may be more accurately phrased "how did I get here?" While it certainly presents plenty of challenges, it's the easier of the two questions to reason about in tangible terms.

We've already begun to break "how did I get here?" down into "from whence came the body?" and "from whence came the mind?", and we'll continue to travel along these two parallel veins. We'll be delving deeper into the origins of our physical selves here. I said we would be starting at the bottom and working up, but beginning with our observations is something like finding ourselves on top of a partially built structure and trying to figure out what we're standing on. In that sense, we've looked at it from the top down so far, but as I hope you'll remember from the first chapter, it isn't enough to scratch the surface. Whatever the answer to the question is, we will need to go all the way down to the foundation. So it isn't enough to ask "what caused me?", since that question will inevitably beg the question "what caused the thing which caused me?"

Obviously we'll save ourselves quite a lot of time and trouble if we skip as many intermediary steps as we can, and instead examine the "First Cause." This First Cause has been a puzzling conundrum for philosophers for nearly as long as there have been philosophers to be puzzled by conundrums. It's an intuitive question; if we walk backward from where we are, it's where the trail ends—which is to say it's where the trail begins. But it's worth asking, as many have, whether there needs to have been a beginning at all.

There certainly doesn't seem to be any apparent end to the stream of time as we experience it. Anyone who has ever watched the clock during the last hour of a day at school or work, for example, has gotten a disheartening glimpse into the interminable infinity of the future. If time, as far as we can tell, is unending as we move forward, there's no obvious reason why it couldn't extend indefinitely into the past as well. If life, time, and space are anything like what they appear to be, though, then the question can't be answered quite so simply.

Existence in this universe, as we experience it, is a sequence of events. It's a progression from one event to the next. There are moments, followed by moments, in what feels like an endless stream. You can look at this process in terms of notable events, like birthdays or the various milestones we pass as we grow, or break it down as finely as you'd like into the smallest theoretical instants. Incidentally I'm on a plane as I write this, traveling hundreds of miles per hour. If I were to see on a map where I was, even by the time light could bounce off the map and hit my eyes so that I could become aware of that fact, my location would already have changed slightly. There is something so fleeting about a moment, but it is important to notice that there is also something discreet and distinct about each moment.

The fact that I'm never aware of where I currently am (only of where I just was) makes the present seem transient and immaterial, but there's still an order to the events. I was at location X, then just afterward I was aware of that location, even as I reached a different point in space. An event (or a set of concurrent events) occurred, then another event, followed by another. In one moment there was a state of being, in the next a different state. No matter how infinitesimal they might be, these moments are distinct from one another, which means they're quantifiable, which in turn means we have a problem with an "infinite history."

The trouble is that if I had to wait for an infinite number of moments to pass before I reached the one I'm currently experiencing, then I would never be done waiting, which means I would never have experienced this moment. Or put another way, if I have to wait an infinite number of days before I reach today, I'll never reach today. Infinity, by definition, is always unfinished. Nothing can happen after an infinite number of seconds or minutes, because an infinite number of seconds will take forever to pass. Forever never ends, so nothing can come after it.

To some this may seem too abstract for practical purposes, but it presents a real problem from a naturalistic perspective. If history has to have been finite, then how did time begin? What came "before" time? Or really the question is what existed "outside" of time, since the idea of "before" is meaningless in an existence without time. If time, which along with space makes up the fabric of this universe, is anything like what it seems to be, then it would take something outside of the universe to explain its existence. None of the natural laws of chemistry or physics work without time. Whatever explains the origin of time, it isn't those.

Now remember what I pointed out in the last chapter, about how the mind seems to be only loosely bound to time. It would be very easy to overstate the connection between the two points, but it's worth mentioning again here that the body is inextricably bound by time, just like everything else that makes up the natural universe. The mind is the only thing we know of which seems to be able to exist somewhat detached from time. We can't draw anything conclusive from this of course, but to me it seems very reasonable to suppose that whatever this thing is which exists outside of time, it is probably more like a mind than it is like anything else we know of.

If discussing time directly is too abstract for your tastes, though, there's a more tangible way to think about the way causes work in the context of history. It goes back at least as far as Aristotle, and begins with the observation that things are in motion. As Newton astutely observed, an object in motion will remain in motion, and an object at rest will remain at rest, without some kind of external influence. There isn't any kind of matter in this universe that we've observed which moves of its own volition. Things always move because they are acted on by some force; anything that I see which is in motion was moved by something else, and will continue to move unless something else stops it.

If I didn't bore you into drifting off while reading what I wrote about time, you may already see where I'm heading. With movers as with moments, someone has to pay the tab eventually. You can say that C is in motion because of B, and B is in motion because of A, but you can't go back like that indefinitely. It's impossible for there to have been an infinite chain of movers, because if an infinite number of objects needed to be moved before the things we see in motion today were moved, they wouldn't be moving. Forever never ends. There must have been a first mover, and it must have been different from all of the other moving things we see around us. It must be able to explain its own motion, without referring to anything outside itself. It must be, as Aristotle put it, an "Unmoved Mover."

If an object remains in motion unless disturbed, though, you might wonder what if this "Unmoved Mover" was simply always in motion? But if we consider what it really means to have been moving forever, we realize we've really only rephrased the problem.

It's difficult to really grasp what infinity means, for me at least. I seem to be able to imagine an object which has been traveling undisturbed forever colliding with something else, but really I'm picturing the object at the "end" of its journey. But of course if its journey had an end, then it wasn't really infinite. Mathematically, if an object moves infinitely in any direction, it will be infinitely far from everything else in the universe. The idea that it could collide with something after traveling forever seems conceivable, but only because we're unable to clearly imagine what infinity is like. In trying to get around the problems with infinite causes by invoking infinite movement, we're fighting fire with fire. As you might expect, all we're likely to end up with is more fire than we started with.

To some, all of this may sound too abstract to be useful. It's true that we've had to examine time and motion in broad strokes, but even a careful, scientific attempt to explain the universe confirms that the principles are sound. Scientists, many of them naturalists, have been grappling with the same problems as the philosophers and have reached many of the same conclusions.

Entropy is the problem, in a nutshell, from a scientific perspective. Heat, for example, if undisturbed, always moves from areas of highest concentration toward the areas of lowest concentration. Extrapolate that into infinity, and you end up with a universe where heat is evenly distributed. Such a universe would have no points of concentrated energy (like stars), and certainly no life as we know it. While the idea of a "steady state" universe was apparently popular in the 19th century (despite its failure to address the entropy problem), it has been more or less ruled out by modern cosmologists. The most accepted models put the age of the universe at around 13.8 billion years old. I've stated before that I think we're very often overconfident in estimates like that, but the point is that most cosmologists now agree that the universe had a beginning. It's easy to miss exactly how important that is.

If the universe had a beginning, then it had a cause. Even if you reduce the universe down into a singularity, with all of the matter that makes up the galaxies around us compressed into a single infinitesimal point, where did that singularity come from? You might say that it has simply always existed, but then why did it explode into the universe we see today? Who lit the fuse on the big bang? Space cannot be extrapolated indefinitely backward. Time cannot be extrapolated indefinitely backward. There must be something which exists outside of space (as we know it) to explain why the universe is expanding. There must be something which exists outside of time (as we know it) to explain how time began.

As soon as we acknowledge the possibility—let alone the probability—that something beyond space and time exists, the foundations of what many of us were taught in school about the universe begin to crumble.

As far as anyone can tell, the universe began, and yet every part of it which we've observed is contingent, which means the view supported best by the evidence is that something fundamentally different than the universe must exist in order to explain how the universe came to be. By definition that thing must be supernatural; the natural laws all depend on space and time. And if there must be such a thing as a force or entity which is able to create a young universe, why not an old one? If there is something which can explain how the big bang happened, how can we say with any confidence that it couldn't have caused a universe which already contained stars and planets, and somehow given them all a push? For that matter, how can we say with any confidence that this force only interfered once?

I mentioned earlier how theists are sometimes criticized for using a "god of the gaps" as an ad hoc explanation for things that haven't (yet) been explained. What many seem to miss is that the same criticism applies equally to the other end of the argument. It isn't inherently any less reasonable to suggest that a being explains the unexplainable than it is to suggest that a natural force explains it. Both are completely uneducated guesses as far as empirical observation takes you. No one was taking any measurements of the speed of light or the gravitational constant 500 years ago, let alone 13 billion years ago. A god of the gaps certainly deserves criticism, but only as much as a natural force of the gaps.

The heart of the problem is that while how we *could have* gotten here might be legitimately posed as a scientific, or perhaps mathematical question, how *we did* get here is really a historical question. And as you can imagine, history that predates historians is devilishly difficult to learn about. When we speak of the problem as solved because we've found one possible explanation we're affirming the consequent (if you remember what that means from several chapters ago). Saying that any of the various cosmological models floating around the current scientific zeitgeist is the correct one—when all we can really say for sure is that it's one possible explanation of some of the facts—requires an enormous leap. Given what we know, the only truly reasonable answer to the question "what was happening 13 billion years ago?" is a shrug and a pair of raised eyebrows. If there was anyone wandering around in the condensed space that supposedly existed then, apparently they weren't considerate enough to jot down any notes for us. An educated guess is as close as we'll ever get without some form of time travel. All we have to tell us now are the faintest echoes and dimmest shadows. Empirically, the evidence is insufficient.

There's no way to know that the speed of light hasn't changed since the beginning of the universe. There's no way to tell if the force of gravity has remained constant since the dawn of time, or even whether it's the same in some other galaxy. And the fact that there was a dawn of time, that the universe must have had a beginning, demonstrates beyond any doubt that there's something we don't understand. There's something at play which defies our entire collective understanding of the natural universe. We may not even be able to fully imagine what that thing is, let alone observe it.

Albert Einstein said "One thing I have learned in a long life: that all our science, measured against reality, is primitive and childlike - and yet it is the most precious thing we have." I'm not sure I quite agree that it's the most precious thing we have, but if anyone has ever been qualified to make an assessment of our collective scientific achievements it was Einstein. We talk about eons of prehistory as if we know what happened—as if we know anything was happening at all—but if we're honest, all we have are shots in the dark. There are at least dozens of naturalistic theories, and as many or more supernaturalistic theories. In the end, the only means we have of deciding between them are philosophical rather than empirical; no one was around to make any observations.

It's an unsatisfying answer, if it can be called an answer at all. We're left with the necessity of a First Cause, but only the barest descriptions for it (or "them," I suppose, but Occam's Razor would have us prefer a single cause). It must somehow exist "before" time. It must somehow exist "outside" of space. We have no way of knowing if it triggered the big bang, or created a universe with matter and light apparently in transit just before we entered the picture. If it did command the beginning of the universe, we have no way of knowing if it has interfered with the natural order since then—or if it might do so ten minutes from now, for that matter.

It isn't much to work with, but it's something. In order to explain ourselves, we need something which exists beyond time and space. We need something which is not contingent on anything else for its own existence, which is to say something that is fundamentally different from every natural thing we've observed. We don't know much about it from the echoes and shadows which reach us from before the earliest historians, but whatever it is, we can at least be sure it's extraordinary.

The trouble with minds

The idea that the body can't be explained in natural terms certainly carries profound, albeit vague, implications. But as we've mentioned, the body is only one part of a person, and not even the most important one, really. If the body can't be properly explained in natural terms, there doesn't seem to be any reason to expect that the mind should fare any better. We can at least examine the question of where the body comes from scientifically; we can take measurements and extrapolate. The mind gives us exactly nothing to work with from a directly empirical standpoint.

We can measure electrical signals between neurons that certainly seem to correlate with the thoughts we have. If I decide to think about something, it very often results in predictable patterns of physical activity in my brain. The part that's impossible to measure is why I decided to think about that thing in the first place. Of course the process is often inverted, sometimes the signals in the brain precede, or even bypass any kind of willful, deliberate thought, but the important thing to note is that they are different things. By definition, truly willful thought could never be the result of an aimless process. What I mean by the mind, as I hope I've already made clear, isn't the brain. If you can explain the body, it's at least very likely that you will have explained the brain along with it, but even if you've explained the brain, that doesn't necessarily mean you've explained the mind.

A few chapters ago I illustrated the process of transforming truth into knowledge as crossing a rickety bridge over an ominous chasm. I mentioned there how it was a nearly hopeless task, and that it was worth noting how amazing it is that we were able to cross the bridge at all. What makes it amazing is that there's no real reason to expect that it should be possible.

There are two facts which I think might be surprising to someone who hadn't been born into this universe. The first is that the universe is deeply intelligible. The second, and perhaps the more profound (certainly in this context), is that we're able to understand it. The fact that science and mathematics are possible—that even the things which seem to be chaotic are generally following rules or patterns on closer inspection—is really extraordinary. If the universe simply happens to be the way it is, then the way it works is arbitrary. It's anyone's guess why there should be an ordered universe, with physical principles and predictable interactions, where two plus two always equals four, as opposed to one which was in constant chaos. If it's a strange coincidence that the universe merely happens to be comprehensible, it's stranger still that we can comprehend it—and both of those pieces are necessary to explain reason.

The fact that your mind is capable of reasoning is already well proven if you've understood this sentence. That access to reason is the specific property of the mind that makes it so difficult to explain without invoking something outside of nature. I would even go as far as saying the fact that your mind can reason puts the idea that it's explicable in purely natural terms to rest.

It might be prudent to pause here and clarify what I mean by reason. As far as I can imagine, there are two possible kinds of reason. The first is what I'll call "genuine" reason, which is what most of us suppose reason to be. I can imagine a different kind of reason, though, which only seems to be genuine. If inference weren't really discovery, but simply the mind traveling along the only path it could have taken given the circumstances —like a stone rolling down a hill—then explaining human reasoning (if you could still call it that) would be a far easier task. Whatever the mind was, if it were simply mechanical, if it merely deterministically followed some pattern, it would be easier to believe it were derived from some unknown kind of natural force. If that's all reason is, though, then it's merely the "illusion" that I referred to a few chapters ago. By any practical definition of the term, it ceases to be reason at all.

We know intuitively that a non-rational cause for any thought invalidates it for the pursuit of truth. C.S. Lewis points out in his book Miracles how often we say things like "he only thinks that because he was born in such and such a place," or "she's only saying that because she's hungry." If what's driving someone's thinking is a thing devoid of reason, like a geographical location, or the time since their last meal, we no longer take it seriously as "reasonable." This is because real reason requires a decision. If I'm not actually deciding what I believe, then I'm not actually discerning between what's true and what isn't. And if what's determining my course of thought is a mindless, random process, bound only by physical (or even metaphysical) principles which simply happen to be, then I'm left with little but a fool's hope of reaching the truth. Any accurate belief I hold at that point can only have been reached by a practically impossible coincidence.

Computers use exactly this kind of "illusory reasoning," and some might argue that the fact that they're able to reach valid conclusions refutes what I've just said, but there's quite a bit more to it on closer inspection. Once a computer has been programmed, it will respond predictably to any given input. Some see artificial intelligence as an example of a purely physical kind of reasoning, but that viewpoint misses the very important role of the programmer. A computer can do exactly nothing unless it is given instructions. As someone who has worked for years as a software engineer, artificial intelligence is, to me, a misnomer—or at least its meaning is often broadened well beyond the scope of what a computer can actually do. A computer can "learn," which is to say it can effectively make inferences, but in every case it isn't the computer that's done anything that looks at all like genuine reasoning.

A programmer can write software that does something very complex using a comparatively simple set of instructions. They can tell the computer "success looks like this," and "failure looks like this," and the computer can compile measurements while iterating through whatever routine the programmer specified. Eventually, using mathematical algorithms against the compiled data, it can produce predictions or note patterns (even ones which a human being might never have detected by themselves), but it didn't do any of those things by reasoning for itself. All of the reasoning happened before the computer did anything, when the programmer specified "success looks like this." The "if, then" statements were all given to the computer by the programmer. It didn't—and couldn't—establish any links between facts of its own accord.

Science fiction is rife with stories of artificial intelligences which surpass and supplant their creators. While those outlandish scenarios are generally implausible, I can't confidently say there's no possibility of some dialed-back version of those stories happening; it may very well be the case that some day a computer's memory will contain more knowledge than the entire human race. If it does, though, it will be because a human being told it "this is what knowledge looks like," and "this is how you distinguish between true and false." A system so powerful and complex that we can't accurately predict what it will do is theoretically possible, but that is due to our limitations, not the system's transcendence. In fact, we fail to accurately predict how a computer program will respond to a given set of inputs all the time, it's what is known as a software "bug." But whether we get the prediction right or not depends on our ability to reason, not the computer's. Given a set of instructions and physical circumstances, no matter how complex the system, what a computer does will always be the only thing it could have done.

Since we believe ourselves to be capable of reasoning, we must either be creatures which are, in fact, capable of reasoning, or ones which can't trust their own minds. The latter leaves us at a dead end regarding knowledge of any kind, so the only possibility worth considering is that we are indeed reasoning creatures. If we are capable of reasoning, then there are two possibilities which follow that could allow our reasoning to be called valid, and only one if it can be called genuine. Either we are not like the computer, and we are actually free to decide what we believe, in which case our reasoning is genuine and therefore possibly valid, or we are like the computer, but we have been "programmed" by someone who imparted to us the ability to discern between true and false, in which case our reasoning may be valid, but it's a mere imitation or expression of some external reasonableness. For our purpose in this chapter it makes little difference which one, since in either case, whether we were somehow bestowed with genuine reason or merely set down a predetermined reasonable path, we're left with the necessity for a reasonable cause.

If we're left needing something outside of space, something outside of time, and something reasonable, the picture begins to look more and more clearly like a mind—or at least more like a mind than anything else we know of. We can take it a step further, though, by examining a particular kind of reasoning, namely moral reasoning.

Before we dive too deeply, we need to establish what "moral reasoning" actually means, and we'll have a difficult time doing that without establishing what morality is in the first place. I would be hard pressed to fit a proper exposition on the nature of ethics into the latter half of a single chapter, but there are a few noteworthy points of interest that we can briefly discuss, which are pertinent to the task at hand. I recommend the first several chapters of C.S. Lewis's Mere Christianity for a more thorough treatment of the subject, but I'll cover what I can in the space I have.

There are three main branches along which ethical inquiry usually travels. The first is the view which most of mankind has held for almost all of recorded history, that morality is a "natural law"—which is to say that it is something that exists independently of our understanding. Right and wrong are concrete concepts that apply equally to everyone (although those in power have often insisted that the "right" thing to do was what served their own purposes). Those who hold this view might, for example, say that murdering an innocent person is objectively wrong, no matter who the murderer is—even if the murderer doesn't happen to agree with that moral principle.

The second branch suggests that morality is merely a social construct. Some have even gone so far as to suggest that the idea of "natural law"was invented as a means of subjugating the masses. As with any other category of belief (since by definition it must apply to a category of believers), while we can identify a starting point, ultimately this belief can travel in many directions as it's drawn to its conclusions by individual thinkers. Some go as far as positing anarchy as the only reasonable moral framework, while others suggest that this social contract should be upheld—in some form or another, for some reason or another. Nietzsche, for instance, preferred ambition and pride ("master morality," as he called it) over kindness and empathy ("slave morality"). He thought the question was unimportant, though, and his only real justification for his assertions was his own preference, which he seemed to believe was itself merely a byproduct of intricate, mindless causal chains. It's worth noting that whatever specific form this belief takes, personal preference is all you're left with in the end. If there is no moral reality, there can be no statement that correlates with it. Without a moral reality, there can be no moral truth.

The third branch, which has become increasingly popular in my lifetime, attempts to take a middle road by suggesting that morality is real, but that it is subjective. What may or may not be "right for me" depends on "my truth." We discussed at length how subjective truth (which includes subjective moral truth) is a mirage that quickly fades on closer inspection. A true statement must correlate with what is real, so in order for me to make a true moral statement, there must be, in some sense or another, a moral reality. It can't be merely a statement about my preferences, or my proclivities. If what I mean when I say "this thing is wrong" is really "I feel an aversion toward this thing," and what I mean by "this thing is right" is really "I feel an inclination toward this thing," (or at least no aversion toward it) then I haven't said anything about morality at all, I've merely informed everyone of my own feelings. It may be a perfectly true statement about my feelings, but that doesn't make it any more or less valid as an ethical pronouncement.

In practice, the problem is that unless you begin with the first branch, any attempt at a moral framework invariably ends up smuggling in some objective ethic which it can't explain. If morality is a social contract, for example, the whole system hangs on it being wrong to break that contract. Otherwise you haven't established that murder is wrong, only that it may be unpleasant if you're caught. If you assume it is in fact wrong to break the social contract, you may succeed at reducing morality to a single moral truth, but that truth still can't explain itself.

There have certainly been individuals who have taken all objective ethics off the table and embraced the hedonistic anarchy that remains, but while an individual might be able to live that out, a society never could. If everyone used only their desires and urges to govern their actions, society would implode under the weight of injustice and ultimately cease to exist as we know it.

And moreover, it's only a tiny minority of us who don't seem to be innately aware that there are things which we should and shouldn't do. Across all of history, there are certain threads that run through every society we know of. Things like courage, fidelity, and selflessness are almost universally present in the values of peoples separated from each other by continents and millennia.

One might suggest that if a "moral society" (which abides by those universal virtues) benefits the species, and self-preserving behaviors are "naturally selected," then perhaps you could explain our innate inclination toward certain moral principles naturally. Explaining morality this way, though, leaves you with more questions than answers.

The first gap is that not all of the values which we find so prevalent have any discernible biological utility. For example, marriage, in some form or another, has been present in every culture we know of, even those which could have had no contact with one another. A monogamous person is substantially less likely to produce offspring. From a purely biological standpoint, adultery is beneficial to the survivability of species. One would have a hard time condemning other sexual crimes as well, as people who tend to perpetrate them would also tend to produce more offspring. But nearly anyone who reads that sentence will immediately be aware of how callous and, frankly, evil it sounds to suggest that there may be some excuse for sexual crime.

There are plenty of other examples of virtues which are practically universal with no apparent biological benefit, like self-sacrifice, or courage, or generosity. All of these seem to fail to contribute to—or even hinder—the survivability of an individual, or otherwise limit their ability to reproduce. There is no justice for the cruel in nature. The fittest survive, usually at the expense of those weaker than themselves. Those hindering traits like compassion and generosity are certainly admirable in a mate from our cultural context, but remember you have to explain the biological purpose of that admiration as well, or you'll have the cart before the horse. Almost anyone would rather start a family with a good man or woman than a bad one, but that doesn't go very far in explaining why we think them good or bad in the first place.

The second problem is that while we seem to have this innate knowledge of what is right and wrong, we don't always do the things we believe we ought to do. Natural selection has been suggested as a means of explaining behaviors, but it can't directly explain the beliefs that drive some of those behaviors, and much less so the beliefs which are contrary to our behaviors.

If we assume mainstream naturalism, this discrepancy between our beliefs and our behaviors must be the byproduct of some random mutation that has survived throughout all of recorded history (and presumably much longer since it is found almost universally in the entire species) despite the behaviors being very often counterproductive to our capacity to survive and reproduce. "Only the good die young," as they say. We should expect humanity's intuitive view of morality to look very different if it were driven purely by biology. When we look at the instincts we have—and indeed which many animals have— which benefit the group at the expense of the individual, we're at a loss to explain them. It should be the tyrants and the cowards that survive, while the gentle and valiant are martyred for the greater "good." And if that's true, then you would expect the ethical progress hypothesized to explain our moral proclivities to be a regress instead. Through that lens, our world looks less like a senseless thing becoming good, and more like a good thing slowly becoming senseless.

And most of us can feel that "regressive" animal instinct within ourselves. The desire to take, when you know you should give. The desire to run, when you know you should protect those weaker than yourself. Those desires are at war with something, and it's that something which seems impossible to explain biologically. If it isn't given to us by our DNA, though, the only viable alternative is that when we have moral ideas (especially those common to our entire species) which are at odds with our baser instincts, we are actually participating in some kind of shared moral reality that exists outside of our selves.

Really the question is framed by one we've already answered. In fact, whether or not it's probable that moral beliefs are driven by blind natural process is mostly beside the point. Even If moral beliefs have somehow permeated our species biologically in defiance of natural selection, they are entirely different from the kind of beliefs which are the result of a genuine decision to adopt an opinion about reality. More broadly, as we've said, any belief (moral or otherwise) that is the result of mindless, reasonless natural processes can never itself be truly reasonable. Here again, it's the brain versus the mind. If the brain is where morality comes from, it's no different than the impulse to eat a sandwich or scratch your rear end. It can never be any more or less than any other biological impulse— which is to say it has no moral value whatsoever. In the same way that there's no rationality in feeling hungry or tired, there's no rationality in simply feeling an affinity or aversion to a moral action or idea. You can certainly engage reason in how you react to that feeling, but whatever you do about it after the fact can't help you explain the feeling itself. If it comes from the brain, if it's merely electricity and chemistry rolling down the hill blindly, it cannot actually be reasonable in itself.

If morality begins (for us) in the mind rather than the brain, however, then the possibilities are much more interesting. Either it is a nearly universal delusion, or it is really an observation of the "natural law" spoken of by philosophers from Aristotle to Rousseau. What all of this boils down to is something which isn't obviously an important question to modern minds, though it should be. Is morality real, or isn't it?

Nearly everyone believes that it is real, in practice if not in theory. If you cut a philosophy professor off in traffic as he's leaving a lecture about the nonexistence of objective morality, I'm willing to bet that he would condemn you for your lack of concern for his personal safety well before he remembers that he doesn't believe there's any legitimate reason you should care about it. There are very few people who are truly devoid of compassion (at least I don't think I've met any) and, inversely, I don't know of anyone who isn't at least somewhat offended when compassion is lacking in a given situation, especially (but not exclusively) toward themselves. Whatever philosophical principles a person prefers, nearly everyone is willing to wholeheartedly condemn things like genocide, and rape—even cutting in line, for that matter. Even if it is very often overcome by circumstance or by other competing impulses, the functional belief that some things are truly right, and that other things are truly wrong, exists in nearly everyone. If it's merely a biological impulse then it's no use condemning Hitler or Stalin; they were simply following their own impulses. It would be like someone who preferred apples being outraged at someone who reached for an orange instead. But if those moral beliefs which we find within ourselves are actually grounded in something real, it must be something real in a different sense than the physical universe. The physical universe simply won't do as an explanation. Without some sort of moral reality which is accessible to our minds, the question of how many of our moral beliefs come to us must remain a mystery.

What all of this amounts to is that nature fails to adequately explain moral reasoning, and more broadly it fails to adequately explain any kind of reason, and thus it fails to explain the mind. If this is true, it must mean that there is something inherently supernatural about the mind. To the modern thinker, that term generally invokes the fantastic and mystical, but my meaning here is much more mundane.

"Unnatural" might be a better term in some ways, although that brings even more unhelpful connotations. I'm using the word supernatural in a more literal sense to simply mean "above" nature. Or it may be more useful to think of this supernatural component of our minds as behind, or below our natural experience, holding it up and giving what we see and touch meaning that it couldn't otherwise have.

Because, really, that's where meaning exists; it cannot exist apart from the mind. Music is just noise, unless it was purposefully constructed by its composer. A painting is just pigment on a canvas that happens to reflect light a certain way, unless a painter decided they wanted to capture a special moment, or convey a message. There is a trend I personally find rather annoying in modern art (although I may just be misunderstanding the intention altogether), wherein artists abdicate from "interpreting" their own art. To me this renders whatever expression they intended meaningless. Or you might say it fails to be an expression at all, really. If you didn't make any decisions pertaining to your art, then it wasn't an artistic expression, it was merely a thing that happened. But of course the artist can never really remove themselves from the equation, there must at least have been a decision that whatever accident they observed was interesting enough to share with the world, and even that small shred of intent is enough. Intent is the key difference between a meaningless accident and a meaningful expression. Both can be beautiful, but truly meaningful things are never really accidents; meaningful things require intent by definition.

That question of intent is really at the heart of everything we've discussed about our origins. A purely natural universe, guided only by blind forces which simply happened to exist, and which is devoid of genuine will, could never produce anything reasonable, let alone anything that reasons. If there is anything truly meaningful about this universe, it couldn't have come from nature itself. We have this habit of personifying nature, calling it our mother, or saying that it's cruel (largely depending on the weather, in my experience). But really, nature can never be anything like a caring mother, or a cruel mistress. In either case it would have to decide what was valuable to it, and that's something matter and energy are fundamentally incapable of doing.

Here you may, like me, find yourself somewhat at odds with the barely acknowledged observations that incline us to think of nature as a person in the first place. It does seem, at times, very much like nature provides us with exactly what we need. In fact it does this in a way that seems inimitable despite our best efforts. "Processed" foods are generally less conducive to good health than what nature has already produced. Try as we might, we haven't come anywhere close to creating anything like even a single cell (let alone a macrobiotic organism). Our deliberate efforts to reproduce what is provided in nature typically fall well short of what supposedly happened by accident. One would suppose that even billions of years of accidents shouldn't be able to produce what thousands of years of deliberate attempts couldn't. It's the old metaphor of a tornado rolling through a junkyard and assembling a working vehicle. The odds of it producing anything remotely useful—let alone precisely what is necessary—are absurdly slim. And yet here we find nature teeming with interrelated systems so complex and varied that even a single microorganism puts our most advanced machinery to shame.

This is strange enough to make all of nature seem absurd, barring a single possibility. A mindless force relies entirely on probability to create anything, and as far as we can tell the odds against life as we know it simply coming to exist are effectively insurmountable. But the only alternative to a mindless force is some kind of intelligent force, and if we assume an intelligent force behind nature, probability ceases to be a factor. That is to say the only way it isn't extremely improbable that nature would provide exactly what we need is if that's precisely what it was *intended* to do.

So we must explain a mind which transcends every natural thing we know of. We must explain its access to a moral reality which is felt, but leaves no significant empirical trail for us to follow. We must explain how a universe exists which is far more intricately interdependent than anything we could have imagined.

The core of all of these ideas, and really of any question of origins, is the concept of creation. Nature can create, in a sense, but it is limited by the tools at its disposal. Matter and energy, given time, can certainly become different kinds of matter and energy, but never any more or less than what it was to begin with, and only ever by sheer, dumb luck. And even then only given a set of circumstances (like the force of gravity) which themselves must be inexplicable accidents. A mind, though, is free of those shackles. A mind is capable of intentionally creating something genuinely new, and distinctly different from itself. As I write this book, the atoms being rearranged in my computer are fundamentally no different than they have always been, but I make willful decisions with every word I chose (and then often regret those decisions and try the sentence over again). Simply by making those decisions I'm creating ideas, and those ideas are distinct from my mind itself. The atoms I rearrange, and the letters on a page that will be produced from the information they hold, are an altogether different sort of thing than those same atoms randomly arranged, even if they happened by an uncanny coincidence to take the same shape. Even if the atoms have been around for untold eons, the idea they contain is a truly novel thing.

One might argue that ideas seem to share the same ethereal sort of reality that minds themselves occupy, so perhaps this form of creation (a mind creating ideas) may be no different than nature "creating" natural things. That is, perhaps new ideas are just the rearranging of preexisting mental stuff. The difference is that by some means or another, my mind is able to interface with nature and use it to intentionally create natural things which wouldn't—or perhaps even couldn't—have existed without its influence. While my mind is not itself a natural thing, unlike nature, it is able to exceed the bounds of its "realm," and willfully reshape other forms of reality.

This property of the mind makes it utterly unique among everything we experience and observe, and provides a possibility which illuminates all of the questions we've been asking. Nature cannot explain itself, but a mind-like thing needn't be contingent like the natural things we observe. And since we know at least one mind-like thing—the human mind —is able to interface with and manipulate nature in a creative way, a mind-like thing which exists primarily untethered to this universe could conceivably explain both itself and the universe as we know it.

We ended the last chapter in need of something which is itself beyond time and space, and yet capable of bringing them into existence. As we close this chapter, we're left needing a "supernatural" cause for the mind. We're left needing to explain how that mind can be reasonable, when reason, as far as we can tell, isn't a natural thing. We're left needing to explain how the moral reality we observe came to be. We're left with a universe which has all of the hallmarks of being deliberately designed. Phrased succinctly, the only answer which satisfies all of these needs is something which exists fundamentally beyond space and time, is intelligent, and capable of both creating material things and defining good. In the immortal words of St. Thomas Aquinas *"et hoc dicimus Deum"*—and this we call God.

As far as I can tell, every other attempt to answer the questions we've asked requires us to invoke something which is either impossible or so absurdly improbable as to be practically impossible. Without a Being which is distinct from the universe itself and has the capacity to reason, we cannot explain ourselves. We have no basis for supposing an omniscient, omnipotent, supernatural Being to be inherently probable or improbable. Since He would need to be a Being who vastly transcends our own intelligence (at least I've never met a human being who figured out how to create a physical universe), we have no way of suggesting that if He existed He would behave a certain way, or that His creation should look like one thing or another. But when we look at everything we have observed on a cosmic scale throughout all of human history, and at everything which we know must be true simply by merit of the fact that we exist as thinking creatures, the most reasonable explanation is that Someone did, in fact, paint the sky.

Other useful tips

If you're coming here after skipping the last three chapters, you may want to skip a few more paragraphs. I have a bit more to say about God before moving on to the real meat of what I'd like to say.

But assuming I have succeeded in reasonably examining these questions of origins, to what does all of it amount? Remember we've discussed that finding one possible solution, even the most probable one, doesn't mean we've arrived at a proven conclusion. Even after having considered all of these trains of thought, and dozens of other very convincing arguments (see the works of St. Thomas Aquinas, G.K. Chesterton, C.S. Lewis, Dr. John Lennox, and countless other authors and speakers who are much cleverer than I am), I'm hard pressed to say that I know concretely that God exists purely as a result of rational inference. I can only arrive at it as (by far) the most probable conclusion. Remember what we said when we talked about the mind and its relationship with reality, though. I can almost never be completely sure, but I can certainly be sure enough.

Because of what must be true, and what that truth implies, I am sure enough that God exists. I am as sure that God exists as I am of anything else I believe to be true. I am sure enough to write it down and present it to a world that often scoffs (or worse) at believers. I am sure enough to live my life according to principles that others might find pointless, if not foolish.

And part of the reason I took the time to write the last three chapters, and to tell you the truth as best I'm able, is that if I'm right, we live in a completely different kind of world than many of us suspect. Things which are created intentionally must be considered in an entirely different way than things which simply happen to exist. Things which are created can be meaningful, and that changes everything important about them. Their beauty is a different kind of beauty. Their purpose is a part of the thing itself, as much an attribute as its color or size.

Moreover, it follows that if we are created beings, we must think about identity in an entirely different way. Instead of attempting to define ourselves and determine our value based on what we like, or where we were born, or who our forefathers were (all of which must boil down to mere accidents if we aren't created beings) we have an objective point of reference. I touched on this briefly a few chapters ago, but I'll repeat it here: if we simply happen to exist, our intrinsic worth is questionable at best. But if there is a being powerful enough to speak things into existence, and that being says that you are beautiful and precious, then the final word has been spoken on the subject. I could write an entire book on the difference between created beings and accidental ones—in fact I might if anyone bothers to read this one.

There is, of course, quite a bit of distance between the loose outline of a Being that we've established and the God of Christianity in whom I've professed my belief. I don't have the space here to close that gap but truthfully there are so many insightful and brilliant writings on the subject, like C.S. Lewis's "Mere Christianity," or G.K. Chesterton's "Orthodoxy," that I doubt there's much I could say on the subject that hasn't been well said already.

Suffice it to say that the Judeo-Christian God fits the bill we've outlined in the last few chapters better than any other idea of God, and the figure of Jesus (both historically and philosophically) is absolutely unique, especially if you're willing to look closely. But as this book draws to a close, it's a different point I hope I've made—or it might be fairer to say I wasn't as interested in making a point at all as I was in trying to help you make your own points.

This book was never really meant to prove that God exists, or to prove that Christianity is a belief system that's coherent with reality. While I believe both of those things to be true, what I really hoped to do, and what I now hope I have done, is to establish a paradigm where we can have a productive conversation. I've used what I feel is the most important conversation largely as an example, though I hope it gave plenty of useful context and relevance to our examination of truth. What I hope I've given you is a means of seeing through and beyond rhetoric and apparent gray areas. Simply put, I hope I've given you the means to decide for yourself whether or not anything in this book was worth paying any attention to.

I mentioned in the preface that what I'm really responding to is the cultural climate I find myself in. It's an era wherein truth is often shelved in favor of simplicity and comfort. Paradoxically, this has resulted in a culture that, to me, seems to be incredibly complex and uncomfortable. The problem is that denying truth its place, like practically every other attempt to take the easy way out, results in benefits that are very short-lived.

I mentioned before that objective truth enables us to bridge the gap between otherwise isolated minds. In that sense truth is the foundation of any genuine relationship. This means that while you can dismiss truth to avoid a difficult conversation with someone close to you, and you may feel better for a day, you'll invariably find the relationship ceases to grow. If you make it a habit, you'll find an inevitable shallowness in all of your relationships. If an entire generation makes it a habit, you will find billions of people who are fundamentally incapable of understanding one another because they have lost their frame of reference, and thus any hope of a truly meaningful relationship.

I can't speak for everyone, of course, but many of the people I know, and certainly most of the people and characters I encounter in the media seem quite content to dodge the fundamental questions. There might not be any practical problem with that, except that they aren't content afterward to dodge discussions which depend upon the answers to those questions. How can we discuss race, gender, or abortion without having any frame of reference for what a human being is in the first place? How can we discuss whether one law or another is just, without having any frame of reference for what morality is to begin with?

We have cut ourselves off at the legs. First because, of course, we can't have productive conversations about the implications of the answers to the important questions without answering them. But it has a much broader effect, because a tower without a foundation is severely limited in the heights it can reach. We have crippled our ability to deal with practical problems like government and interpersonal conflict. If all answers (or no answer at all) to the deepest questions are to be considered acceptable, we must politely insist that knowledge stand on its head. Instead of examining reality to discover truth, we must begin with "truth," and expect reality to fall in line—an idea which reality doesn't seem to care for. We have built our tower on nothing but sand. It should come as no surprise that it relentlessly threatens to topple over. Clearly we don't all agree on the answers to the important questions, but we simply cannot move forward without admitting that while people who agree aren't always right, disagreement only happens when at least one party or the other is wrong. Of course we may still collectively choose the wrong foundation, but any foundation is better than none at all.

I think some may read that last paragraph and think of me as callous. It's easy to speak of the necessity of difficult conversations theoretically without doing justice to the immense emotional weight that is carried between two parties which disagree. In my culture, though, and in most of the modern cultures I'm aware of, we have compounded the weight of that burden enormously—and unnecessarily—by suggesting that saying someone is wrong is somehow antithetical to loving them.

Part of the problem is tied up in what I mentioned earlier in this chapter about how we see identity. We seem to have a habit of bundling our ideas, beliefs, and even our preferences into who we believe we are. The trouble is that if we conflate a particular belief or preference with a person's identity, then the lines become blurred between disagreeing with an idea, and disagreeing with a person's very being. But if my identity is rooted in something deeper than geography and social happenstance, who I am has little to do with what I like.

In order to discuss this meaningfully, we must make a distinction between "who" a person is and "what" a person is. Who I am is distinct from what I am—the things which make me a person are different than the things which make me a mammal. But while we all know that there is a difference, it's intuitive and difficult to put into words. The simplest way I can think of to describe it as it seems to me, is that "who" a person is refers to the parts of them which make deliberate decisions, whereas "what" a person is finds its definition in a person's circumstances.

As it pertains to our ideas and beliefs, there's no obvious way to decide which thoughts you have are a direct result of your "true self," and which ones you're only having because of your situation or experiences. In effect it boils down to the age-old "nature versus nurture" debate, and there's a reason that debate has yet to be settled. There's obviously no truly scientific way to tell the difference, since you can never put the same person through two different upbringings, but I'm inclined to believe that it's almost never entirely one or the other. There are things you will do because of who you are, and other things you will do because of where and when you were born, and probably most of the decisions you make will take elements of both into account. There is this apparent duality within us, there is a "who" and a "what," and I think that sense which nearly all of us have—that we are more than our bodies—is confirmed by what we've discussed about the difference between the "natural" things bound up in spacetime, and our minds. There is certainly a part of us which is physical and is bound by spacetime, and there is another part of us which doesn't seem truly bound by the physical universe at all. The latter part is the "who" (or so it seems to me, anyway). When we talk about who we are, as opposed to what we are, I believe we're implicitly referring to our minds, not our brains.

Let me explain what I mean. Have you ever had an object which was so comfortable and familiar that it almost felt like a part of your body? Like a baseball glove, or a favorite pair of shoes. Or if you have a good amount of experience driving a car, that might be a better analogy. When you're driving and you want to stop the car, you don't think "I need to push the brake pedal with my foot so the car will stop." You simply think "stop" in the same vague sense that you think about moving your hand to your nose to scratch an itch, and the action is carried out with very little mental effort. In a sense you "become one" with the car—you're no longer thinking about the car as a set of objects, you're simply thinking about what you want to do and almost instinctively making it happen. And though a bump in the road does nothing to affect your body directly, you "feel" it in almost the same way you feel pavement under your shoe when you're walking. It's a dulled and diffused sensation, but your mind interprets it almost as if it were your body touching the road directly, and not the car. The car, in a sense, becomes an extension of your self, though never truly a part of your self.

Now if you take a step back, it seems to me like that same sort of operation is happening within our bodies. Obviously none of us can remember what it was like, but I imagine that for an infant, learning how to move one's body intentionally is very much like learning to drive a car. It's very easy to feel like my body is intrinsically a part of who I am, but perhaps this is due almost entirely to the fact that I have never been outside of my body (at least as far as I can remember). After you've been driving for a while, you're hardly aware of the car anymore. It's only when you begin driving, and when you decide to stop driving and get out of the car, that it truly feels like a foreign object. I imagine if we were able to decide to stop "driving" our bodies, we would realize that there's something foreign about them as well.

Now we know about this distinction between our true self and our bodies from practical experience. If Dave loses an arm in a tragic accident, he isn't fifteen percent less Dave than he was before the accident. We know this because when we communicate with him it's clear that we're talking to the same person we spoke with before. What's less clear from anecdotal evidence is whether a change in one's brain changes who they are.

This question, incidentally has some fairly personal relevance in my life today. The father of some friends of mine fell from the top of a building and suffered a nearly lethal head injury a few months ago. He's still struggling to recover most of his memory from the last several years, and has even forgotten who some of the important people in his life are. As it pertains to this question, in suffering damage to his brain, has he suffered any damage to his identity? I think most people will have the same instinctive answer to that question—a resounding "no, he has not." At least as far as all who know him are concerned, he is still the same person he was before the accident. The same father and husband, the same friend and family member to those who love him—even if many of his behaviors and attitudes are different than they were.

Again, none of this can really be confirmed in any concrete way, but it makes sense when placed in the context of the larger picture we've been discussing. If you step out of the car, you realize it's a foreign object, despite feeling connected to it while you were driving. It follows that one's body is very likely the same—losing a part of it doesn't diminish the person, only the "vehicle" they were driving. In the same way, I would contend, the brain is simply a vehicle employed by the mind in order to interact with the physical world, and is subject to all sorts of chemical and electrical imbalances and imperfections which have no bearing on a person's true identity.

The reason that's important is because when we draw a line between a person's "true self" and their brain, we draw a line between an entire class of thoughts and the person's identity. With that line drawn, the only thoughts which have any real connection with a person's identity are the ones which willfully guide the brain, not the ones which are guided by it. It's the difference between a person running over a mailbox because their tire blew, and a person who steered into it deliberately because they wanted to ruin Mrs. Johnson's day by scattering her mail all over the front lawn. The former has no bearing on who they are, while the latter almost certainly does. If the brain is the vehicle, and not the driver, the driver's identity is unaffected by the particulars of how their brain functions, even if those particulars may have a powerful influence on their behavior.

This has several implications which are pertinent to deciding whether disagreements should be equated with offenses against a person's being. Firstly, any type of thought that's guided by a physically-driven preference is immediately invalidated as an extension of a person's being. My preferences toward things like food or weather become detached from the "who" part of my self, and relegated to the "what." What I do about a craving may have some bearing on who I am—if I decided to steal some food I liked from a grocery store, for example—but the craving itself is simply a result of how my vehicle's steering is aligned. And if that's the case, how we treat the decisions and opinions of ourselves and others must be different than if we wrap all of the biologically driven thoughts we have up in a person's identity. It requires us to recognize that many of the opinions we have are likely influenced by our circumstances, and thus likely do far more to identify our environment and culture than they do do identify ourselves.

I'm sure it must have happened at least once your life that you have changed a belief you had because you realized the reasons you held the belief weren't really based in anything other than the fact that you found something (or someone) to be either attractive or off-putting. There are people who make careers out of manipulating brain chemistry to get people to do or believe what they want. I would argue that it isn't fair to judge the character of the victims of such manipulators for their coerced actions (very harshly, at least), since those actions were largely the result of their circumstances skewing their mind's attachment to reality. It is fair, however, to judge the character of the manipulators, since they willfully decided to take advantage of their victims.

Obviously the lines can't be drawn quite so distinctly when examining the thoughts and behaviors that straddle the border between "true self" and "natural," or perhaps "animal self." It's very unlikely (or at least it seems unlikely to me) that many of our beliefs are purely a result of willful deliberation, and are not "corrupted" by our circumstances. At least I can say for my part that it takes quite a lot of work to separate the subjective "truth" and the objective truth. Here's where the warnings I've repeated about how we consider things we hope or fear are true really come to a head.

It is hard to quiet the internal voice that seems bent on reconciling the brain and mind. If your brain is telling you that something is good, your mind seems to try and justify its goodness to make sense of the signals it has received. All of the times your brain has accurately relayed information goad you into relying on it more heavily than you should. It's something like a malfunctioning gauge in the metaphorical vehicle. If the gauge says the fuel tank is full, you won't assume you need to do anything to continue driving safely. You'll be disinclined to pay any mind when the engine begins to stutter, or other lights appear on the dashboard. In the worst cases you'll find yourself in a very precarious position before you realize what the gauge reported wasn't reliable.

Fear can work the same way, in the opposite direction. When we're afraid, our bodies send all sorts of signals, and when those signals reach our minds, especially for those of us who have suffered some sort of tangible trauma after receiving those signals in the past, it's often difficult to believe that it could be a false alarm—even though it very often is. I think most people will find they've been afraid much more often than they've truly been in danger.

These two forces of desire and fear, attraction and repulsion, are in themselves mindless. They may generally behave a certain way in relation to reality, but they are most often ultimately a result of chemistry and physics. They are not drivers, merely components of the vehicles we drive. The trouble with having components like these, though, is that our vehicles, like any other vehicle with unreliable gauges and mechanisms, can sometimes be practically more of a hindrance than a help when it comes to getting where we need to go.

That has two important implications for our purposes. The first is that grace (to use a Christian term), or something very much like it, is a necessary component of productive conversation. It is of paramount importance to understand how truth works on a fundamental level, just as it is of paramount importance to understand the rules of the road when driving, but it's foolishness to think any of us will ever follow those rules flawlessly. And there is no reasonable place for either judgment or pride when it comes to how anyone drives their vehicles, because no one chooses the means they must use to navigate this life. A very good driver in a very bad vehicle may still be beaten in a race by a very bad driver in a very good vehicle—especially if you're only looking at one stretch of the track. A person can't be blamed for having a bad vehicle, only for how they drive the one they have. And inversely, while a certain amount of credit for maintenance may be due, a person who has a good vehicle which they neither chose nor paid for, has no business being haughty about how much time they spend on the road instead of in the bushes.

The second implication which is important for our purposes is that if a person's incorrect beliefs may be merely a symptom of their vehicle's faults, then there's nothing morally wrong with being factually wrong, and nothing morally right about being factually right. Getting something right that someone else got wrong may certainly make one *feel* superior, but for all anyone knows they may have only succeeded in using a sports car to beat a half-working old pickup truck in a street race. That certainly doesn't give any meaningful indication of their skill as a driver. And what would be the point in being proud (or ashamed) of one's skill in the first place? Lacking experience, or development of a given skill can hardly be held against someone who simply needs training, nor can having skill be truly taken as merit toward someone who's simply further along the path we all must tread.

If any of this is true, it means that when two people disagree, while it's true that the quality of their beliefs, in a sense, may be disparate, this has hardly any bearing on the quality of the believers. Once one is willing to admit that premise, we're able to separate the idea that a person is wrong from the idea that a person is "less than" in any regard. A person can very reasonably say "I dislike your ideas" without in any way saying "I dislike you." Now there may very well be some correlation—at least I've found that the more of a person's ideas that I disagree with, the less likely I am to feel an affinity toward them—but in any case, a person should be held no more responsible for disliking someone than they are for liking them. This may have more to do with the vehicle than the driver, as well. It isn't reasonable (or productive) to hold a person's dislike against them, as it's generally beyond their control. Nor is it any credit to a person to dislike bad things. If a person feels an aversion to the actions of Stalin or Hitler, that isn't any credit to them; they didn't choose those feelings. It's only a credit to them if they deliberately decide not to be despotic or murderous in their own lives—and as far as that goes, they probably deserve more credit if they do feel an affinity for despotic action, but choose to act with kindness and generosity in spite of it.

I spoke of humility as the only reasonable response to the smallness of our understanding as compared to the scope and breadth of truth. I said there that this reasonableness imbued humility with a certain usefulness. We find here more reason for it, and thus more use. There is no reasonable place for pride in one's ideas or beliefs, and inversely no place for shame. In the vacuum left by the absence of pride and shame, humility takes its place as the only sensible alternative. What I mean here by humility is simply the recognition of oneself as a limited creature among other limited creatures. You will get things wrong. Others around you will get things wrong. There will be times when it is completely beyond your control whether or not you get a thing right, and there are places you may not be able to reach in the vehicle you drive. Some may know more, some may know less, but no one will know everything. Knowledge, then—by which I mean a genuine understanding of truth—is not a badge of honor, but a privilege. If you have it, you're no better, though you may be better off. If you don't have it, you're no worse, though you may be worse off.

So disagreement is inevitable, but it is often merely the collision of struggling drivers in vehicles which are hopelessly unfit for the journey they must take. If we're able to keep this in mind, and brace ourselves accordingly, these collisions needn't be anywhere near as painful as they often are. If one is able to adopt an attitude of respect and compassion toward each person they disagree with, and approach each discussion with the understanding that either party might be wrong for reasons which are ultimately beyond their control, the sting of a disagreement is drastically reduced. It's the difference between receiving a negative comment directed toward my wife's car, and one directed toward my wife herself. The former might vaguely annoy me, while the latter might bring out a significantly less civil response. If my reaction to both is the same, it's because lines between the two which should have been sharp have become blurred. If we're collectively able to sharpen the lines between what a person is, and who a person is, we'll have much more success relating to one another in a productive way.

Even if we make the distinction clearly, though, while we can reduce the friction and heat of disagreements, the only way to truly avoid that pain entirely is to stop disagreeing, which is clearly a lofty goal. In fact, it seems likely to me that it is impossible (in our present state of being, at least), but that certainly doesn't mean it isn't worth striving toward agreeing as often as we can. Here is where the kind of truth whose existence I spent thousands of words trying to prove truly shows its worth.

Imagine two ships are sailing, and wish to sail together. There are a few ways they might achieve this. Obviously if they both choose a direction independently of the other, there's a much better chance that they'll grow further apart—or collide —than there is that they'll sail along together. The first viable way to sail together is that they each aim toward the other. That will certainly bring them close together, but what are they to do once they reach each other? They'll end up chasing each other's tails and going nowhere in the end. The second way is that one ship makes the other ship its target, while the other chooses a destination. That will certainly work to an extent, they'll avoid collision, but it robs one ship of its autonomy, and furthermore if they both travel at the same speed, while they won't get farther apart, they won't get any closer together either. The only way they can both travel together, while maintaining some degree of freedom, and yet avoiding collision, is if they both agree on a destination and aim toward that fixed point. That way the longer they travel, the closer they'll get to one another, and yet never collide.

This is the way people relate to each other ideologically. Except instead of two ships sailing in an open ocean, it's more like billions of ships crammed into narrow channels. The principle is the same, though; any ships which haven't agreed on a destination are either robbed of their autonomy, or bound either to collide with one another, or drift off into isolation. If we want to give each person freedom, but avoid colliding or drifting apart, we must decide together on a fixed point we can aim toward. Nothing that's relative to the heading and location of any one ship will do, without an inevitable sacrifice of autonomy for the other ships. Truth—objective truth—is the only feasible candidate for that fixed point. The only viable way for us to live harmoniously together is if we can find a way to genuinely agree on what is objectively true. Anything less will be a poor substitute. Agreement is far more valuable than many of us realize. It is worth striving toward, not simply to avoid the unpleasantness of a disagreement, but because of the enormous power of a harmonious human race. Because of the freedom truth brings, to move alongside each other without collision, and to reach a place worth going instead of aimlessly wandering.

So, in light of all this, here are my suggestions. I hope you will find them useful.

Take truth seriously. And then take it lightly. Do your best to understand what truth is, and then let that understanding permeate the way you think about everything, from your work to your play, from your business plans to your romantic fantasies. There is certainly a vast and important space for creativity and wonder—for dreaming about what might be—but truth enriches everything it touches.

Build your foundation. Take the time, at least once, to ask the deepest questions. Challenge every assumption, both yours, and, as much as you're able, the ones held by the people you're listening to. Make sure you know what supports an idea before you lean on it, and you will find yourself able to build higher and higher as your foundation becomes more and more solid.

Seek true knowledge. Don't settle for "facts," search for truth. Don't merely try to remember what you're taught, try to understand it. There's no point in remembering what you were taught in school, or what you learned watching a documentary if the thing you remember isn't true. Continually ask yourself "how do you know?" If you ever find yourself unsure of how to answer that question regarding something important, then dig deeper until you truly understand. Don't take anyone's word (least of all mine) for the answers to the really important questions. You'll have to do the work yourself, but in the end you'll have built something that no one could have built for you.

Seek wisdom. Once you have knowledge, do something with it. Otherwise everything I've tried to show you in this book will have been for nothing. Apply knowledge, connect it, and use it to improve your life, and the lives of those around you. If you discover God, learn what His existence really means. Knowledge for its own sake is nothing, but when it is applied it becomes a force to be reckoned with.

Have the hard conversations. Disagreement can be a terrifying thing. It's nearly always uncomfortable, and there are even some with whom disagreeing is tantamount to declaring a war of words. But unfortunate as it may be, a disagreement is often the only viable avenue toward an agreement, and an agreement is a beautiful thing. You will very often close that avenue, though, if you forget to approach every disagreement with humility, and a gracious willingness to treat the person you disagree with as a human being who is no better or worse than you are for having reached a conclusion you did not. But if you are willing to truly listen, and have trained your ability to see to the heart of a matter and determine what must, or cannot be true, you have an opportunity to bridge an otherwise unbridgeable gap. If you have discovered truth, it will benefit you. If you share that truth, it will benefit others. Disagreeing with someone who believes a lie, then, is not doing them a disservice; it is inviting them to share in your freedom. And you may find in the process that they are in fact the ones equipped to share freedom with you instead. But if having a genuine conversation is too intimidating, do what I do: write a book expressing your disagreeable beliefs, and then, after enough people have read it, listen as intently as you're able to what the angry mob is yelling as they wave their pitchforks.

Certainty is an elusive thing. It may even be beyond our reach. Perhaps Socrates had it right, and the wisest among us is simply the one most aware of their own ignorance. But if you'll allow me to leave you with one thing, let it be this: be as sure as you can about everything that matters. Take the time to think, and then, once you're sure enough, do something with what you've learned. Help those you can help. Read, listen, learn, and when you discover the truth, share it with anyone who will listen.

Thank you for listening.